Enjoy!

Claudette Burnett

Murderous Intent?

Long Beach, CA: 1880's-1920

Claudine Burnett

authorHOUSE®

AuthorHouse™
1663 Liberty Drive, Suite 200
Bloomington, IN 47403
www.authorhouse.com
Phone: 1-800-839-8640

www.claudineburnettbooks.com

First published by AuthorHouse 3/27/2009

ISBN: 978-1-4389-4044-1 (sc)

Cataloging-in-Publication Data
Burnett, Claudine E.
Murderous Intent? Long Beach, Ca. 1800's-1920 / by Claudine Burnett.

p. cm.
Includes index.
1. California, Southern – History. 2. Long Beach, Calif. – History.
3. Murder – California – Long Beach. I. Title.

979.495 – dc21
F869.B94 2009

Printed in the United States of America
Bloomington, Indiana

This book is printed on acid-free paper.

I

In memory of those whose stories are told here

Contents

Introduction

This book is the result of eighteen years of researching local newspapers during the course of my job as a librarian at Long Beach (California) Public Library. Others who contributed include fellow Long Beach historian Judi Cameron, whose editorial comments helped greatly, Rose Katsuki of the Long Beach Police Department and Todd Houser of the Long Beach Police Historical Society, who tried to find police records relating to the cases. I'd also like to thank my husband, Paul, and my many friends who have politely listened to these stories and encouraged me to write this book as a legacy for future generations interested in Long Beach history.

Why did I decide to write about murder? History should be interesting. What better way to cloak the story of a city than with a subject that has always aroused morbid fascination? Ever since Cain slew Abel, there has been something about the act of taking another's life that makes us want to learn more about the causes behind such drastic action. Today, unfortunately, murder seems a common occurrence, but in Long Beach's early history murder was a rare event. In the years spanning this volume, the 1880's to 1920, less than 35 actual murders occurred in the Long Beach area. Yet I found many compelling stories, recounted in the book, where murder could have been the end result.

Was "murderous intent" involved in these cases? I'll leave that up to the reader to decide.

Some of the accounts told in this book may seem incomplete. Was the murder suspect ever captured, tried or sentenced? Unfortunately, Long Beach police records only go back to 1944. I have provided as much information as I've been able to find through newspapers and other sources. I have chosen to footnote only direct quotes with the newspaper name and date, since Long Beach Public Library's entire *Long Beach Newspaper and History Index* has been used as my resource guide. A bibliography for these tales can be found in Long Beach Public Library's online *Long Beach History Index* at www.lbpl.org. A subject or keyword search will lead you to representative articles.

Murder and Alcohol Kill a City

1894 was a pivotal year in Long Beach history. It was the year that murder arrived in the city. Not one, but three murders in the same year. Long Beach would never be the same.

Who would have thought that murder would come to the idyllic seaside village nestled along the Pacific? Long Beach was a quiet town, known for its religious conventions and temperance views. Crime was almost non existent, though there was something that most villagers thought was criminal, and that involved town founder William Willmore.

It wasn't that Willmore was dishonest, just the opposite, he had been so fair in his dealings with those who purchased property from him that he wasn't able to pay his debt to Jotham Bixby, the major owner of the Rancho Los Cerritos on whose land the town had been founded. In 1882 Bixby had sold Willmore and his investors 4,000 acres of Los Cerritos land (NOTE: The original map & ads said 10,000 acres purchased, later this was reduced to 4,000 acres).

Willmore had been unable to pay either of the first two installments called for in his contract with Bixby. Instead he spent the money he made to improve the 350 acre town he named Willmore City and the surrounding farmland known as the American Colony. He had promised investors to bring in water, sewers and lighting, and he lived up to his word. As June 1, 1884 approached, the date for making the final payment on the $100,000 purchase price, Willmore realized he couldn't pay, and relinquished all claim to the property. What had happened to this honest man *was* criminal, locals who remembered him claimed.

Disheartened, Willmore went to Arizona. There, it was said, he suffered sunstroke which seriously affected his health. Later he returned to Southern California a pauper. Unable to work and support himself he became an inmate of the Los Angeles County Poor Farm. Ironically, if Willmore had been able to hold on financially to his new town a little longer he would have been a success. A tremendous land boom hit Southern California in 1885 when the new transcontinental Santa Fe railroad was completed. A price war developed between the Santa Fe and the older Southern Pacific, with tickets from Chicago to Los Angeles falling from $52.50 in 1883 to $4 in 1886. Thousands moved to the Southland, many of them to the former Willmore City, which now boasted a new name—Long Beach.

By 1894 most people traveled to Long Beach by rail on the Terminal or Southern Pacific railways; it was only a short ten minute ride east of San Pedro. Once here visitors were treated to a beautiful beach, a pavilion, bath house, swings for the children and small pavilions placed along the bluff for picnickers to enjoy the great ocean view. The school census taken in the spring showed the year-round town population to be around 1,000 people, but during the summer the population swelled to between 5,000 and 6,000. About 30 new residences were built that year, along with a number of small summer cottages. There wasn't much for Long Beach City Marshal Kinman to do except deal with tourist complaints and the peculiarities of some of its citizens.

One of the most talked about locals was "Whistling" Davis, a Long Beach farmer, who was decidedly eccentric. According to neighbors the

60-year-old, 6-foot tall farmer was miserly, overbearing and egotistical. Davis and his family migrated from Kansas in 1885, purchasing forty acres in the Willows development at Long Beach and twenty acres on the mesa near Signal Hill. Davis had been in trouble with the law on several occasions: once when he drove an agent of the Horticultural Commission off his farm with a shotgun when told to spray his fruit trees; another time for tearing out a gate in an irrigation ditch. Mrs. Davis, it was said, frequently feared for her life. Her husband would not let her go anywhere or allow any neighbors to visit. He also had an eye out for any passing boys who purposely taunted him by whistling or singing. Davis would rush out swearing and shoot in the air to scare them away. This hate of whistling had earned him his nickname "Whistling" Davis.

The talk of the neighborhood was Davis's keeping his dead child's coffin on his porch, denying her a decent Christian burial. In 1890 Davis's two-year-old daughter contracted cholera. Through ignorance or a mistake an overdose of paregoric was given the child. As the youngster got worse a physician was sent for. The doctor said he could save the child's life by using a stomach pump, but Davis would not allow it and the doctor went away and the little girl died. Following his daughter's death Davis's behavior became even more bizarre. He wouldn't allow the child a regular burial saying the cemetery proprietors wanted too much for a burial plot. Instead, he dug a shallow grave in his potato patch and buried the coffin. Two years later he dug the coffin up and put it in his cellar. It stayed there until the cellar flooded and his other children rescued it and placed it on the porch. Since then the tarnished casket had sat on the Davis's front porch, in plain sight of the family and passers-by.

The scandal about the coffin and Davis's alleged ill-treatment of his wife and family came to the attention of county officials. When the deputies investigated they found the coffin containing the dead child's remains partly concealed under the porch and called the Long Beach coroner to come and open the casket. Inside they found the emaciated body of the child. Mrs. Davis, who a *Los Angeles Times* reporter said did not appear to be very bright, believed it was her husband's intention to clean the bones of the child and put them away. She explained she didn't know whether he intended to keep the coffin to use again should one of the other four children die. In any case, the coroner confiscated the casket and put Davis under arrest on the misdemeanor charge of failing to provide decent burial for his child.

Though Davis' refusal to allow his child medical treatment was "murderous" in most people's opinion, he had not actually taken her life violently. But it was the thread that began to unravel the serenity and peace the town had enjoyed since its founding. Trouble was brewing in Long Beach, trouble that would end up killing the city.

1894 became known as the "Year of Murder," among Long Beach folk. Not just one, but three murders had taken place all in one year. Of the three, one occurred on the Rancho Los Cerritos, one on the Rancho Los Alamitos and the last one in the town itself. Though Long Beach prided itself on having five religious organizations in town and only one saloon, drunkenness was the cause of two of the murders. Many just shook their heads, saying they should have *never* allowed a saloon in town.

Willmore and his successors, the Long Beach Land and Water Company, had wanted to attract the very best class of people to their community and create an environment where children could grow up without any "contaminating influences." In every deed there was a clause binding the owner of the land never to sell, permit to be sold or give away intoxicating liquor. In September 1886 a Mr. Pickering opened a saloon about one mile from the center of Long Beach at

Atlantic and Anaheim. Being out of the town limits he didn't worry about city restrictions on alcohol. One of his customers was a young man from Visalia, Missouri, who couldn't control his drinking and died with an empty whisky bottle under his pillow in a Long Beach boarding house. This enraged the Long Beach Women's Christian Temperance Union and they quickly arranged a mass meeting of the whole community. Emotions ran so high the entire town marched to the saloon, voiced their complaints, and presented a paper to Mr. Pickering to sign. It read:

"Mr. Pickering - Sir: At a citizens committee meeting held at Long Beach tonight, it was resolved that the assembly wait upon you and request from you a positive assurance that you will immediately cease your nefarious business of liquor selling and close your saloon by 9 o'clock tomorrow morning; otherwise we, as citizens of Long Beach, warn you that a warrant for manslaughter will be issued at once for your arrest and conviction. Do you promise? If so, sign this paper and we depart in peace."
(LA Times 10/13/1886)

Pickering was only too glad to sign, for while the agreement was read to him a rope was placed around the saloon and several men with horses stood ready to pull the building down should he hesitate to sign. By daybreak the contents of the whisky shop stood in the street ready to be moved far away from Long Beach. The people of Long Beach rejoiced in their victory and vowed to stop any saloon going in anywhere near their town.

But that had been in 1886, two years later the city incorporated *and* it needed money. On March 2, 1888, Long Beach formally organized its city government and elected John Roberts president of the Board of Trustees. One of the first official acts of the Board was to pass an ordinance prohibiting saloons, gambling houses or other institutions "dangerous to the public health and safety." A property tax rate of .50 cents on each $100 assessed valuation was established. However, many property owners could not be located and more than 400 lots were sold for taxes at the end of the year.

By May 1890 the Board of Trustees faced with a depleted city treasury and a number of illegal "blind pigs," as saloons were called then, made a controversial decision. Their one police officer could not or would not do anything about the illegal bars *and* the city needed money. The Board agreed to grant a saloon license to Joseph McPherson for $40 a month, with the stipulation that no tables or chairs be placed in the saloon, that the windows be of plain glass and not curtained, that no card playing be allowed, nor loafing on the premises, and no liquor sold to minors or those who appeared to already have had too much to drink. McPherson agreed and quickly turned his one-story building at the northwest corner of Pine and Broadway from a bakery into a bar. Though all sites in town had been deeded with the stipulation that no alcohol ever be allowed, the liquor ban for this site was lifted by a quitclaim deed.

McPherson immediately painted a large sign on the side of the building which read: "Wanted – one thousand men to unload schooners over the bar." The sign didn't refer to stevedoring, but to the "unloading" of schooners of beer. He was so successful with his advertising that he soon opened a beer garden in the rear of the building. Not all were pleased. (NOTE: there is some erroneous belief that Dennis McCarthy had the first saloon in Long Beach, this was cleared up in Walter Case's *Did You Know That?* column in the Sept. 21, 1932 *Long Beach Sun*).

The granting of a saloon license was to be the pivotal point in Long Beach history, resulting in the disincorporation of the city in 1896.

Had McPherson's saloon led to two of the 1894 murders? On March 20, 1894, the coroner and sheriff received word that a Basque sheepherder, Jean Escunde, had been found dead at Rancho Los Cerritos. Circumstances pointed to murder. The prime suspect, who was arrested for the crime, was Escunde's employer Pierre Pellifigues.

In reconstructing events, the sheriff found Escunde had gone on a drinking binge at McPherson's saloon and returned to the rancho in a very quarrelsome mood. With an alcohol induced sense of bravado Escunde picked a fight with Pellifigues, who had told Escunde he had had too much to drink. Escunde became angry that Pellifigues thought him drunk. Wielding a knife, Escunde attacked his employer. Pellifigues defended himself by hitting Escunde with a club. Escunde managed to stagger to his feet and leave. Pellifigues thought the stagger was due to the alcohol and went to bed thinking all his drunken herder had to do was sleep it off.

The following morning Escunde was found unconscious, his skull fractured from the blow which Pellifigues had delivered the previous night. Escunde died soon afterwards. Thirty-five-year-old Pellifigues, who spoke little English, managed to convey that he had no intention of killing Escunde when he struck him; he had only been acting in self defense when Escunde attacked him with a knife.

The citizens of Long Beach, who knew what alcohol could do to a man, believed Pellifigues and he was released. There was also the fact that they were both sheepherders. Unbelievable as it may seem to us today, the prevalent conviction of the time (reported in the *LA Times* Feb. 6, 1897) was that a sheepherder sooner or later became insane. It was assumed that the constant moving of the flock affected the keeper's brain, eventually driving him mad. Had this been the case in Escunde's death? Perhaps alcohol had muddled the sheepherder's brain even more and was the real murderer? Long Beach residents knew they needed to get rid of the saloon in their town to prevent similar tragedies, but their hands were tied. The Trustees, in desperate straits for money, had issued a liquor license, and they were legally bound to honor it.

Sheep were big business for the Bixby family. Some of their flocks were pastured on the Palos Verdes hills and some on another family ranch in the area of Santa Ana Canyon. During certain times of the year thousands of sheep were driven from the Bixby's Southern California ranchos as far as Ventura County, where the family also owned land. When locals saw huge clouds of dust along Anaheim Road they knew the Bixby sheep were on the move.

By spring the sheep were ready for shearing. A camp was set up and shearers from all over California and Mexico came to earn money. It was at one of these camps, set up on the Rancho Los Alamitos, that another murder occurred less than five weeks after that of Escunde on April 27, 1894.

An investigation revealed that the crime was committed over a very trivial matter. Ricardo Moreno, the murdered Mexican, and his wife had been hired to cook for the sheep shearers on the ranch. On the evening of the murder E. Soto, one of the shearers, went into the cook's kitchen and began slicing off meat from a larger piece. When Moreno objected and told him to eat another part instead, Soto, who had been drinking, became enraged. Wielding the knife he had used to cut the meat, Soto attacked the cook. Moreno raised his right arm to warn his assailant away, but to no avail. Soto cut him with a knife at the lower edge of his arm pit, severing several large arteries and making a gash about three inches long.

The realization of what he had done sobered Soto immediately. He bound up the cook's wound and proceeded to the city of Orange with Moreno to seek medical assistance. But he was too late; Ricardo

Moreno died the next day. Upset and not sure what to do, Soto took off for a drunken binge in Anaheim. He later turned himself in to authorities but told a different story.

Soto claimed self defense, not cold-blooded murder. He showed the sheriff a deep gash in the fleshy part of his left hand and on the left side of his vest, just below the heart, which the young man claimed was made by a butcher knife wielded by Moreno. His shirt was covered with blood and his left hand wrapped in a white cloth. Soto claimed that both the cut on his hand and on the vest were made before he made the fatal pass at Moreno. But had the cuts been made by Soto himself to escape the long arm of the law?

The inquiry into the crime revealed that the victim, Ricardo Moreno, had a reputation as a trouble maker. Four years before his death he was involved in a quarrel with a fellow Mexican in which he cut the fellow's throat from ear to ear. The police in Los Angeles said they repeatedly had trouble with him. Because of Moreno's poor reputation, the involvement of alcohol, and the fact that Moreno had been killed with an ordinary pocket knife, Soto was acquitted of the crime.

Though shocked at these murders, city folk in downtown Long Beach still felt somewhat removed from the tragedies. After all, the murders had taken place a distance from town, on the two ranchos where the spirit of the Wild West still lived on. The third murder to hit quiet little Long Beach in 1894, however, would shock the town to its core. It was seen by many as one of the most cold-blooded murders in the criminal annals of Southern California.

Every evening after closing his business Camille Elikan visited his neighbors, the Lowes, and their daughter, Ethel, who was his bookkeeper and fiancée. The Lowes were prominent Long Beach citizens, who had settled in what was then Willmore City in 1884. Arriving in Los

Angeles from Nebraska, they read advertisements and comments about Willmore City and decided to come and look the place over. The carriage ride to the new community from Los Angeles, however, was so long they decided to spend the night. William Lowe was an asthmatic. When he woke up the following morning he declared he had never slept as soundly as he had in Willmore City. From that moment on the family knew this would be their home.

William Lowe proceeded to purchase some of the most attractive real estate in the townsite. He bought the northeast and northwest corners at Pine Avenue and Ocean. There was a cottage on the northeast corner and this became the Lowe home and the community's first store. A short time later he erected a two-story structure north of the cottage and in 1885, when the post office opened in his store, he became the town's first postmaster. Mrs. Lowe was equally civic minded. In 1884 she started the city's first school in a little frame building at the southwest corner of Pine and Broadway for ten pupils. She also suggested the name "Long Beach" to replace Willmore City as the official name for the new community.

Camille Elikan also found Long Beach a lovely place to live. The town was growing. It was the perfect environment in which to establish a business and raise a family. Here Elikan had found the woman he wanted to marry, Ethel Lowe. The couple seemed made for each other, sharing similar goals and values. In addition, they each possessed a keen business sense, which they hoped would ensure them a secure future. Elikan, with no family of his own, also relished having William and Belle Lowe as in-laws. He and William had much in common; both workaholics with a desire to see their community prosper and grow.

Elikan had a set routine. After closing his store he would sort his day's receipts, place the money in a small satchel and then visit Ethel. The evening of November 22, 1894, was too pleasant to stay indoors so Elikan invited Ethel Lowe for a stroll. She agreed, and he placed his bag just inside the front door of the Lowe's house. The couple returned an hour later, spent another half hour conversing then Elikan left the house with his satchel. A few minutes later Ethel heard voices in the alley and was alarmed at the sound of a pistol shot. She immediately left her room, met her father who had sprung from bed, and asked him to go with her and see what had happened. They rushed to the alley where they saw the body of a man reflected in the light of a street lamp. It was Camille Elikan, still alive, but unconscious. The pair managed to get Elikan back into the house, called a doctor, but to no avail. Elikan died three hours later.

About an hour after Elikan had been shot Lucien Healey and Ethan Feeler appeared on the scene. They claimed they had been nearby, in the cottage where they roomed, when they heard a shot, rushed out and saw a man running down the alley. They said they ran after him, following him to the beach where the man threw a satchel into the ocean. Healey said he continued his pursuit but the man had a horse waiting and rode off. But there were holes in the men's story. Some things just didn't add up.

Realizing that if the story told by the two men was true, they would have had to run at least three miles, William Lowe became suspicious. He suggested to the throng that had gathered that perhaps they should take the men along the route they had described to look for more evidence. The crowd agreed. But in following the men they came upon Elikan's empty bag, which made Healey and Feeler's story even more doubtful. The two men had claimed it had been thrown into the ocean. Under questioning, Feeler caved in.

Feeler said it had been Healey's idea to break into Elikan's store while Elikan was at the Lowe's house. They managed to get in the rear door by removing the hinges. While Feeler watched, Healey went into the store and returned with an armful of canned beef, which they hid beneath the stairs of an adjoining house. They were still in the store when they saw Elikan approach with a satchel in his hand. Healey ran out to confront Elikan, putting a revolver to the storekeeper's head. Elikan placed the bag on the ground and backed away, but when Healey ordered him to walk out of the gate he grabbed the barrel of the gun and tried to get it away from him. Healey then raised his hands and fired. As Elikan fell Healey grabbed the satchel and ran, telling Feeler to follow. When they reached the beach they slit the satchel, took out the money, and then threw the bag into the ocean. They returned to their cottage, changed their clothes, hid the money and mingled with the crowd. They hadn't imagined the satchel would wash back up on shore, revealing no money inside.

Using the latest forensic technology of the day, Lewis Bailey and L.H. Brown took plaster casts of the footprints found in the sand on the beach, and in the alley near the store. They were a perfect match to shoes owned by Healey and Feeler. George Hurst, the local blacksmith, identified the tools found in the two men's possession as tools stolen from his shop. Eventually, both Healey and Feeler admitted the robbery, but each accused the other of firing the fatal shot. Both were sentenced to life imprisonment for murder.

Ethel Lowe was distraught over the murder of her fiancée Camille Elikan, but she became even more upset when a reporter from the *Los Angeles Times* printed a story (Nov. 25, 1894) indicating she was already married to Elikan or had "some kind of partnership with him, or some peculiar authority over his property." People in town told the reporter that Elikan and Miss Lowe were already married and that the matter had been kept a secret. When a *Times* reporter talked to Miss Lowe's mother and asked for a photograph of the murdered man, she pointed to Ethel and said: "She has a photograph, but she will not let you have it. She was his _____." The last word was not spoken, according to the reporter, Ethel's mother catching herself "as if fearful of telling a secret."

The newspaper reported Ethel refused to turn over Elikan's watch and jewelry and took possession of Elikan's business. Elikan's property was estimated at being near $20,000. Why they would have kept their marriage a secret is anyone's guess. Not much was known about Elikan's past. Had he a wife somewhere else?

Ethel would eventually marry Albert Schattman, a local photographer, in the spring of 1898. They moved to Denver, Colorado, soon afterwards; her husband bought a business and she became a mother, giving birth to a son, Max, on July 1, 1899. Unfortunately, Albert Schattman died soon after the birth of his child. When the baby was old enough to make the trip Ethel returned to Long Beach where she died in November 1899. Max was adopted by his grandparents and brought up in Long Beach, the town his grandmother had named.

Murder, it seemed, was contagious. Once it started there was no stopping it. The murderous streak of 1894 continued into the following year. On July 17, 1895, another tragedy associated with drunkenness resulted in murder.

Mabel Meyers feared for her life the evenings her husband went out drinking. The 16-year-old had no idea before her marriage that her husband turned crazy after a few drinks. She should have listened to her mother, who told her teenaged daughter that 21-year-old Alonzo Meyers had a bad reputation. But Mabel was sure her mother was wrong. She was in love. Finally her mother consented to the marriage. But mother did know best. Lon Meyers was insanely jealous of his pretty, young wife. One evening he beat Mabel so severely she could barely move. When she was physically able Mabel fled to her sister's house. Meyers followed and pleaded with her to return. Mabel refused. She was tired of being her husband's punching bag. Instead she decided to take her sister and brother-in-law's offer to vacation with them in Long Beach. The Linsons and Mabel quickly left Inglewood for their summer rental, leaving Meyers behind, or so they thought.

The determined husband followed. The next day he found them in Long Beach. He refused to leave them alone and dogged their footsteps all the way to their cottage on the northwest corner of Elm and First streets, making a scene along the way. Mabel and her sister remained in the yard trying to talk sense into Meyers while Irvin Linson went into the house. Meyers yelled at Linson to come out and talk with him. As Linson approached Meyers drew a revolver and shot Mabel. He then fired at Linson, seriously wounding him in the arm. He then shot at Mrs. Linson, who escaped by running to the rear of the cottage.

Firing another shot into the body of his wife, Meyers then shot himself through the neck, which paralyzed him from the chest on down. When questioned by police Meyers claimed that a man named Frank Doyle had come to Long Beach with Mabel; that he shot his cheating wife twice to be sure she was dead, and that he did not regret the deed. He said Irvin Linson was a gambler who came to Long Beach to open an illicit gambling house with his brother "Kid" Linson and Doyle, also known as "San Francisco Frank." Upon investigation the charge of Mabel Meyer's infidelity proved untrue. Though Mabel had known Frank Doyle there was nothing romantic going on between the two, Mrs. Linson declared. She also claimed her husband Irvin, though a known gambler, had no intention of setting up an illegal gaming parlor in Long Beach. Eight hours after the deed Meyers began to lose consciousness. One and a half hours later he died, without expressing any regret.

The little cottage at the northwest corner of First and Elm, where the Meyers' murder occurred, became the scene of Long Beach's first reported haunting. Hair-raising stories were told in which the spirits were said to come by night and reenact the awful tragedy. No sounds were heard, only the vision of the murder was repeated. Long Beach youngsters walked ten blocks to avoid going past the house at night. Eventually the cottage was torn down and the spectral scenes faded.

Murder continued to stalk the region. On April 10, 1895, word reached Long Beach that Basque sheepherder Juan Gugenburo had been viciously murdered. His killer was Martine Toledo, another Basque sheepherder employed by George Carson, who ran the Dominguez ranch.

The murder was a brutal one, the result of a jealous dispute over wages. For several years Toledo was foreman of Mr. Carson's sheep camp. When Toledo became ill Gugenburo was appointed temporary foreman, but with no increase in salary. Upon his recovery Toledo was reinstated in his old position, but Gugenburo was not happy with his demotion. He had hoped to get Martine Toledo's position permanently. From then on bad feelings existed between the two. Two weeks prior to the tragedy Toledo withdrew all his money from the bank, transferring $55 to Gugenburo's account for the work done during the time Toledo was sick. When the men met at the sheep camp they argued over the $55. Gugenburo did not think it was enough. Toledo said it was all he had. A fight ensued.

A witness said Gugenburo ran from the room pursued by Toledo. Grabbing a piece of nearby wood, Toledo beat Gugenburo over the head with it until Gugenburo was dead. Authorities reported Gugenburo's frontal bone was broken and he had bruises across his chest. His broken knuckles indicated he put up his hands to ward off the blows of the club.

Immediately after the crime Toledo walked to Carson's house, where he got on a horse and rode away. He was later found in Los Angeles where he gave himself up.

These murders, most of which involved alcohol, led to one of the bitterest times in Long Beach history. From the start Long Beach sentiment had been strongly for temperance. But the city needed money to function; citizens didn't want to be taxed, so permitting saloons with a high license fee was a solution. As mentioned earlier, troubles began when Joseph McPherson's saloon, located at the northwest corner of Pine and Broadway, decided to advertise during the 1890 Chautauqua. The Chautauqua, named after Chautauqua Lake in western New York, was a school at home, designed for busy people who never enjoyed a college education; it was open to anyone looking for self improvement. During their summer sessions the various circles which spanned the globe presented lectures and diplomas to graduates. In 1885, with over 150,000 students enrolled in the four year self-study course, the movement reached Long Beach. The city quickly became known as the "Chautauqua City by the Sea." It was Long Beach's biggest tourist draw and the community's largest source of revenue.

McPherson put up a clever banner during the 1890 Chautauqua with a double meaning: "1000 men wanted to unload schooners." This upset the anti-liquor Chautauqua folk so much they vowed to move their yearly sessions to Santa Monica unless Long Beach did something about the alcohol question. Though McPherson agreed to take down the sign, and soon sold the saloon to fellow Irishman Dennis McCarthy, a campaign to put the bar out of business and keep the Chautauqua in Long Beach followed.

Dr. Ervin Chapman, for many years superintendent of the Anti-Saloon League, came and spoke for the dry forces. Women workers for temperance met in the building known as the Tabernacle and prayed for their cause. On July 1, 1896, a new ordinance prohibiting the sale of "spirituous" liquor as a beverage went into effect. It placed the City of Long Beach in a peculiarly complicated situation that would go on for over a year. Opponents of the new ordinance alleged the one saloon permitted in town for the past few years had done little damage. There had only been one case of reported drunkenness. But how many cases of drunkenness went unreported, anti-saloon activists countered? Alcohol was the issue at hand and many remembered the murders of Basque sheepherder Jean Escunde and sheep shearer Ricardo Moreno, all brought about because of too much drink.

The morning of July 1, 1896, Long Beach businessmen found a drape of black crape trailing down the door of every business in town. City trustees who voted for the anti-liquor ordinance were threatened. Trustee William Schilling was approached by a man saying he represented the Los Angeles Liquor Dealers' Association. The man urged Schilling to change his anti-liquor vote or be prosecuted for selling goods to the city and handling city warrants, something not allowed of a city official. Schilling replied he had nothing to fear, that he was elected on a temperance platform, and he could not vote in favor of licensing a saloon.

The threats made by the Liquor Dealers' Association were carried out. On July 8, 1896, Long Beach saloon owner Dennis McCarthy filed a suit against certain Long Beach Trustees. The title of the complaint was "The people of the State of California, upon the accusation of D. J. McCarthy vs. K. Almind " The document stated that on April 13, 1896, the defendant, Kildorf Almind was elected to the office of Trustee of the town of Long Beach. That while a Trustee, it was his legal duty to refrain from becoming interested, directly or indirectly, in any contract with the town. The accusation went on to state that on or about May 15, 1896, a Mr. Townsend was employed under a contract with the Trustees to grade Pine Avenue. While doing the project he used Almind's horses and wagon; he also used the services of Larcom Teale, agent and employee of Almind.

Dennis McCarthy also brought suit against William Schilling. He stated that ever since Schilling was elected Trustee on April 13, 1896, he had sold a number of items to the town. These sales were a conflict of interest and illegal because of Schilling's role as Trustee. McCarthy went on to demand that the court award him $500 for acting as an informer.

This was not the end. Another incident involved City Trustee Clarence Coseboom, who was hung in effigy in Pacific Park. Coseboom had run for City Trustee in 1896 and had given his word that he wouldn't interfere with the operation of McCarthy's saloon as long as the business was conducted in an orderly fashion. As soon as he was elected, however, he voted to close the saloon. The next day someone was hanged in effigy in Pacific Park (now Lincoln Park). The straw-stuffed figure which had been strung up during the night to the top of the flag pole bore no name but it only had one leg. Everyone knew it could only be Coseboom who, too, only had one leg.

The City of Long Beach was now without a saloon tax. They needed to raise additional money to keep the town afloat and fight McCarthy in court. Where to turn? Tax the local citizens. A yearly business tax was levied varying from $5 to $25. This tax also applied to small farmers in the surrounding area, and people who rented rooms in their homes.

The anti-saloon advocates of the Chautauqua were delighted at the turn of events. They decided to make Long Beach its permanent home. The Chautauqua lecture sessions held each summer was one of the biggest money makers in the city. Without the Chautauqua and the tourists it brought in, Long Beach would suffer a severe financial loss.

The Chautauqua's threat to move to Santa Monica and pull out of Long Beach completely unless the saloon was closed had greatly influenced the Trustee's decision to make Long Beach completely dry.

But the fight was not over. On July 27, 1896, an election was held to decide whether the city would live or die. Should it disincorporate? If the city was not incorporated it fell under county ordinances, and the county permitted saloons. It was a lively time indeed, with the vote on disincorporation passing by six votes: 132 favoring the drastic measure with 126 opposed. The question of alcohol, it seemed, had killed the City of Long Beach.

But the city would not die easily. On August 4, 1896, the Board of Trustees of Long Beach declared the election null and void. They said the notice of the election was faulty and there was no evidence that all of those who voted were residents of the town. But county authorities did not agree. On August 7th three of the five Long Beach trustees, Kildorf Almind, William Schilling and Clarence W. Coseboom, were arrested on the charge they feloniously refused and neglected to handle the election properly. They were released on bail of $200 each. (The three were eventually acquitted of this and McCarthy's earlier conflict of interest charge). The other two trustees, E. C. Denio and J. C. Dunn said the election was properly handled and the town of Long Beach no longer existed. Municipal Court judges Clark & Van Dyke agreed, declaring the election results to be legal. However, Almind, Schilling and Coseboom appealed the decision to the California Supreme Court.

On September 12, 1896, county supervisors came from Los Angeles and made a formal demand for the public property in possession of the former Long Beach Board of Trustees. Those who contended that the town was not disincorporated put up a lively dispute. What resulted was a refusal to comply with the county's demand.

Until the California Supreme Court made a decision things were in turmoil. Those in favor of disincorporation said the Board of Trustees had no legal right to convene or to pay bills. Dennis McCarthy's saloon, the only one in town, reopened under a county ordinance. This was in direct opposition to the anti-saloon ordinances of the City of Long Beach. Other problems were also arising; who was going to pay the city park gardener and the lighting bill? What was going to happen when the winter rains fell and the pot holes needed filling, culverts cleared, and road crossings repaired?

In the summer of 1897 the California Supreme Court reached a decision. They sided with the Municipal Court verdict: Long Beach was no more. The city was indeed dead. However, some good came out of the case. Because of the problems suffered by Long Beach the state law was changed to require a two-thirds vote, rather than a mere majority, for a city to disincorporate. However, this didn't help Long Beach and the mess it was in.

The once flourishing town of Long Beach was now under county jurisdiction, but the county's ineptitude and lack of caring about the plight of the citizens of Long Beach during this trying ordeal soured many. Citizens in Long Beach decided to resurrect the city and re-incorporate. Petitions circulated, signatures certified and on December 1, 1897, an election was held to determine if the City of Long Beach would live once more. Included on the ballot were the names of officers who would serve on the Board of Trustees if the incorporation carried. The list included names from the Anti-Saloon League and those from the high-license group who favored saloons but with a high fee. The vote for re-incorporation carried by a large margin, with those favoring saloons being elected by a small majority, 167 to 111. As a "new" city, all old ordinances were declared null and void.

On December 13, 1897, the new City Trustees met for the first time. New ordinances were discussed. It was agreed that saloons would be permitted if they obtained a petition signed by a majority of the residents of the town. No minors would be allowed in the saloon, nor would any games, chairs or tables. A saloon license tax amounting to $420 quarterly, and payable in advance, was imposed. On January 10, 1898, Dennis McCarthy's application for a saloon license was granted and the accompanying bond for $1,000 accepted. Peace was not to last for very long.

In March 1898 ardent anti-saloon advocates, most of them prominent in church circles, circulated a petition in favor of complete prohibition. An election was held April 11, 1898. The high-license party swept the ticket with every candidate winning. Saloons were permitted, as long as they paid a heavy tax to support the city. This pleased small farmers, business owners and land lords who would no longer have to shell out a business tax. But the anti-saloon activists were a determined lot.

In January 1900, despite protests from the Law and Order League, the City Trustees renewed the liquor license of Dennis McCarthy, who owned the only saloon in town, for $600 per year. This angered the Law and Order League to such an extent that they gathered signatures demanding another election on the saloon question. On May 21, 1900, the election was held and a no-liquor ordinance passed. The decisively large majority against saloons came as a surprise to many of the townspeople who remembered the liquor situation from 1896, which had led to disincorporation and death of the city. Would Long Beach once again disincorporate? But memories of the ineptitude of county rule lingered. Long Beach had learned its lesson. Whatever might come, the city would survive. However, there was one glitch in putting the saloon out of business immediately. The city, always short of money and not wanting to issue a refund, couldn't put the ordinance into effect until McCarthy's license ran out on July 11, 1900.

July 10, 1900, 11:59 p.m. marked a historic moment in city history—it was the last time you could get a legal drink in Long Beach for many years to come. The ordinance prohibited liquor in any form except upon a physicians' prescription. Those who loved their foaming lager and glass of wine, however, sought safe ways to defy the law. The state legislature had recently passed a bill permitting the organization of "social clubs" behind whose doors members could have a drink or two. Two Long Beach men, a Mr. Cottie and a Mr. Charles, decided to test the new state law out and form a club. Anyone could join the club for .25 cents (which also included the price of a drink). Club members, however, were advised not to mention they were primarily a drinking club; instead they called the bar area a reading room or social headquarters.

The club flourished for a time before the City Trustees took action. When Thomas W. Williams was appointed City Marshal in April 1902 he got busy. Assuming the membership clause of the "club" was a blind and subterfuge to mask the real intention, Williams obtained a search warrant and raided the social club. Liquor was confiscated and the managers arrested. For several days this game was kept up, the clubrooms being raided, then promptly restocked and opened.

The owners tried a new plan. They sent the county sheriff to confiscate the booze, but Marshal Williams threatened to arrest him for trespassing and damaging city property if he tried to take the alcohol. Later a tax officer paid a call on Marshal Williams and threatened the marshal with arrest for having liquor in his possession without a government license. Williams laughed at him. Finally Williams played his trump card. He persuaded the police judge to go fishing, and then he made a final raid on the club. Since the judge was away there was no one to fix bail for those taken in the raid. The prisoners were locked up in a jail so crowded they had to stand. After several hours of confinement the prisoners capitulated and agreed to abolish the club. When the judge was finally located the club managers, on a promise to abandon further efforts to furnish liquor to the city's thirsty, pleaded guilty and were fined $200 each. The club passed out of existence and 1,330 bottles of beer and several cases of liquor were poured out on the vacant lot back of the city hall.

The Wild and "Wooly" Ranchos

In 1849 Benjamin Flint left Maine for the California gold rush ending up in the town of Volcano in what would later become Amador County. Two years later he persuaded his brother Tom and cousin Llewellyn Bixby to join him. They took his word that money wasn't to be found in gold mining, but in trade. Together they built the National Hotel in Volcano while Llewellyn operated a butcher shop and Ben purchased cattle. They became so prosperous that by Christmas 1852 each had $3,500 in gold. They decided to unite their fortunes into the Flint, Bixby and Company and bring sheep and more cattle to California. The trio returned home and enlisted more relatives to join the firm, including Llewellyn's younger brother Jotham. In May 1853 they began their trek back to California with 2,000 sheep, 100 head of cattle, 11 yoke of oxen, 2 cows, 4 horses, 2 wagons, and 3 sheep dogs. They invested in a small mountain farm in Amador County which supplied produce to the miners. Gradually their fortunes increased.

In 1866 the Flints and the Bixbys became the owners of Rancho Los Cerritos, one of the two major ranchos which comprise present day Long Beach. A drought in 1863 and 1864 had caused the death of thousands of cattle and Juan Temple, who owned the Rancho Los Cerritos, sold his land and herds for $20,000 to Benjamin and Thomas

Flint and Llewellyn Bixby. Jotham Bixby was made ranch manager and in 1869 got a half interest.

Austrian Ludwig Louis Salvator visited Southern California in 1876 and described the Rancho Los Cerritos. He wrote that the Jotham Bixby ranch was the most successful sheep ranch in the county. It contained about 25,000 acres, ten artesian wells and 30,000 Spanish merino sheep, each of which could produce about 10 pounds of wool a year. The shearers were all native Californians or Mexicans who received five cents a fleece. One man could shear 40 or 50 sheep a day and as each fleece was delivered to the counter the shearer was given a check worth five cents. Once a week the checks were redeemed for cash. Salvator noted the vast herds of animals in California and remarked that the Spanish settlers never killed a female animal; instead they used them for breeding. He also found it interesting that they would never ride a mare, considering it beneath their dignity to do so.

In 1878 another Bixby cousin, John W. Bixby, leased a portion of the Rancho Los Alamitos. Los Alamitos had become the property of Michael Reese, a San Francisco money lender, when Reese foreclosed on Abel Stearns' mortgage following the drought of the 1860's. In 1881 the whole rancho was purchased from the heirs of Reese by the Bixbys and I.W. Hellman. That same year William Erwin Willmore secured an option from Jotham Bixby on 10,000 acres of Rancho Los Cerritos land for $25 an acre and organized the "American Colony." Willmore's purchase was the beginning of what would become the City of Long Beach.

The July 1, 1883, issue of the *Los Angeles Times* described the Rancho Los Alamitos as "probably the best natural stock farm in Southern California." At the time of the purchase the entire southern portion of Los Angeles County was a swamp of little value. Within five years the Bixbys had drained the water and transformed the southern section of the rancho into the most valuable portion of the 27,000 acre estate. In July 1883 there were 500 acres planted in corn, put in by renters who paid John W. Bixby a share of the crop for the use of the land. There were also 150 acres of alfalfa which thrived on the moist, slightly alkaline soil on the western portion of the rancho. Livestock included 1,000 head of Durham cattle, 8,000 head of Merino sheep as well as 300 milk cows, 140 being milked to supply the Alamitos cheese factory.

Despite all of this farming, the spirit of the Wild West still permeated the ranchos. Southern Californians didn't have to rely on reading dime store westerns to get an idea of the untamed frontier, all they had to do was open the morning newspaper and find real adventure going on in their own back yard. In 1889, for instance, all of Southern California was captivated and somewhat terrified by the actions of Sylvestro Morales, a bandit terrorizing Los Angeles, Orange and San Diego counties. All gave a rousing cheer when Morales was finally caught on the grounds of the Rancho Los Alamitos. The capture was front page news. *Los Angeles Times* subscribers eagerly read how Constable Charles "Keno" Wilson of Oceanside, who had been hunting the fugitive for three weeks, finally trapped Morales and Morales' female companion in the swampy tules at Alamitos Bay.

Wilson had suspected that Morales and his female friend might head for Rancho Los Alamitos. Morales' half sister, Mrs. Sylva, resided at the rancho, and Wilson thought it probable that the bandit would ask her for food and shelter. For several days Wilson hid himself in a barn on a high point of land overlooking the ranch. The barn had a cupola which served as a lookout and, with the aid of field glasses, Wilson and his companion Ypifano Gallego sat back, watched and waited. Wilson had complete confidence in Ypifano Gallego, even though Gallego was a former member of Morales' gang whom Wilson had captured earlier. Gallego had readily accepted Wilson's offer of immunity in exchange for helping catch Morales. Wilson found that Gallego was a man of his word and had won Wilson's trust.

After a few days Wilson observed a woman with a basket coming from the direction of the brush and tules. He was sure she had been taking food to Morales. Not wanting to go into the tules and be at the mercy of a murdering bandit, Wilson bided his time.

A few days later Wilson noticed a man standing in a ditch in the tules a few yards from the Alamitos ranch house, sharpening a knife on a stone. The ditch was deep enough to partially hide the man so that he couldn't be accurately identified. Gallego proceeded to go into the swamp and talk to the man believed to be Morales. While Gallego engaged the fugitive in conversation, Wilson crawled within hailing distance, pointed his Winchester rifle at the suspect, and ordered him to throw up his hands. For several seconds the suspected bandit stood as if considering what to do, finally lifting both his hands as Gallego took away the robber's weapons. When questioned about his female companion Morales pointed toward the brush. There in the marsh was Nymphia Brown, the adopted daughter of Morales' friend Jose Machado. She had no idea that her lover had been captured.

Wilson brought the pair into Long Beach to await the train to Oceanside. Hundreds of people came to the depot to look at the man who had terrorized the whole southern country for so long a time. Morales had nothing to say to reporters, smoking cigarettes and occasionally casting a loving glance at his female companion.

"The career of the bandit reads like a romance," the *Times* reported on September 8, 1889. Morales "seemed to have been born a criminal and lawless character," and for a man slightly over 30 years of age, he had an impressive criminal record. As a young man he was befriended by the Machado family and grew up close to La Ballona, near present day Playa del Rey. Even in his youth he was fierce, vindictive, cruel, and feared by those who knew him. Eight years earlier he had shot a Jewish merchant for some alleged insult. He was sentenced to San Quentin for seven years, stirring up trouble with prison authorities every chance he could. Upon release from jail in the spring of 1889 he went to the New Almaden quicksilver mines in Santa Clara County. He wasn't there long before he stabbed a fellow worker and disappeared. He returned to Ballona, was joined by a man named George Bunch, and together they began to steal horses.

The partnership soured when Bunch stole a horse from the Machado family, the kindly people who had practically raised Morales. Upset at the theft, the quick tempered Morales shot Bunch three times, though not fatally, at San Luis Rey. Morales decided to return the horse to Jose Machado in San Diego. It was the honorable thing to do. Here he met Jose's adopted daughter Nymphia Brown. The couple fell in love and Nymphia eagerly fled with Morales when the lawmen started to close in.

Morales knew the country well. He evaded the posse and made his way to San Juan Capistrano. On August 25, 1889, Henry Charles, a well-to-do San Juan Capistrano rancher, was murdered and Morales was the prime suspect. The whole county became alarmed as Morales escaped to the hills of Santa Ana and Trabuco canyons. Who would be his next victim? An all-out search with an expert posse managed to capture Morales a few miles from San Juan, but he used Nymphia as a shield and got away. Soon after, he was captured at Rancho Los Alamitos.

Meanwhile George Bunch, Morales' former partner, was brought to trial for horse theft and Morales was called upon to testify. Though Morales had returned the Machado horse after he shot Bunch for stealing it, Bunch was still charged with the theft. In addition, Bunch was accused of stealing two other horses from Charles Hawes and A.T.

Stewart of Santa Monica. On September 18, 1889, Morales was brought to Santa Monica to testify against Bunch. Morales, who had already been sentenced to life imprisonment in Folsom for crimes committed in San Diego County, took the stand and swore he had never killed a man, nor was he involved in any horse stealing activities with Bunch.

Bunch was called to the witness stand. He told how he had met Morales in San Bernardino and decided to join him in looking for work in the Los Angeles area. Leaving their horses in Los Angeles they decided to walk to Santa Monica where they stayed with a friend name Chora. Morales borrowed a horse at Chora's, and both men rode it some distance. But carrying two men was too much and the horse soon tired. Spotting another horse in a field Morales went and caught it. At this point Morales gave Bunch his horse and took the other. As they journeyed along a bay filly decided to "follow them," as did a few other horses along the way.

When asked as to whether he knew he was stealing the horses, Bunch answered evasively. He claimed Morales had told him they had been left to Morales by his foster father Soreto Zufias. At this Sylvestro Morales laughed heartily. Bunch declined to examine any witnesses in his own defense. He was fined $6,000 for his crime. Morales was sent to Folsom to begin his life sentence.

In 1909 Morales was pardoned by the governor of California. The good behavior he had feigned in prison was just a sham to achieve his freedom. It was revenge that consumed him. Frequently during his trial he had threatened to kill his captors, Keno Wilson and Ypifano Gallego, as soon as he got a chance. He said he would never rest until he had "squared accounts."

In October 1910 Morales made his way to San Diego and his turn-coat partner Ypifano Gallego. Gallego had settled down to an honest life, raising cattle near San Diego, but his past caught up with him. On

October 14, 1910, Gallego was ambushed and shot. He managed to drag himself two miles to his home, announcing that Sylvestro "Pedro" Morales was the guilty man. He then died. Though both United States and Mexican officers looked for the bandit, they failed to find him.

Morales never caught up with Keno Wilson. A dedicated lawman, Wilson worked as a deputy United States marshal until illness forced him to retire in December 1935. He died on September 24, 1936, at the age of 71.

Throughout California's history as a possession of Spain, then Mexico and finally the United States, Mexican laborers and Native Americans had been the backbone of the rancho's labor force. Hard work was rewarded, regardless of nationality. If you did your job well you might become foreman. It wasn't an easy job. A foreman had to hire, supervise and often fire employees. The hiring was simple; the firing was not, as Juan Acosta, foreman on the Rancho Los Alamitos, discovered.

Just before daybreak on May 8, 1907, Acosta was asleep in his tent, enjoying the last few minutes of a restful repose. The previous day had been hard on him. He had had to fire four men. As foreman on the Rancho Los Alamitos it was up to him to discipline his men and let them go if their behavior warranted it or if work was slow. Alcoholism was often a factor for dismissal and some, hyped up on booze, didn't take being fired lightly, as Acosta sadly found out.

While Juan Acosta slept, the four he had fired the previous day crept into his tent, intent on revenge. They had spent the night drinking at Pete Labourdette's saloon in the nearby town of Los Alamitos, trying to forget that they no longer had jobs. Fired up on alcohol they were determined to "get even" with Acosta for their dismissal.

The light in the tent was poor but Acosta, awakened by a strange noise, could make out shapes in the darkness. A dim shadow moved stealthily closer. Acosta turned in bed just as a knife, meant for his chest, was plunged through his left arm. Acosta started to rise from his cot but was hit with two blows, one to the breast bone and the other to the center of his forehead. Somehow he managed to reach the corner of his tent where he kept his shotgun. Gathering all his strength he picked it up and fired point blank at his assailant. Juan Diaz fell to the floor writhing in agony.

Refugio Acosta, who shared the tent with his brother, scrambled from his cot in a sleepy daze. He wasn't sure if he was dreaming or if his brother was experiencing an actual attack. He sprung from bed and grappled with the nearest shadow, Luciano Morro. The other two intruders, Bartello Rodriguez and Lucas Mendoza fled.

Both Juan Acosta and Juan Diaz were taken to the Long Beach Hospital. Diaz did not survive. Morro was soon captured, but Rodriguez and Mendoza escaped. Juan Acosta was not charged in the murder. No further information can be found on what happened to Morro.

Many laborers traveled from Sonora, Mexico, to work on the farms and ranchos surrounding Long Beach. One of them was Alejandro Banderas. On July 6, 1915, twenty-three-year-old Banderas was shot and killed on the Ables ranch near Artesia. His death was somewhat suspicious, and his murderer never found.

Though Banderas was shot in a tent less than 100 yards from their house, the Ables family knew nothing of the tragedy until twenty-four hours later. Was it a cover-up to let the murderer flee? It certainly appeared so. There were three other Mexican laborers who witnessed the shooting, and other Mexicans living in the area who failed to notify the police. Banderas' countrymen did, however, bring in a doctor who tried unsuccessfully to save Banderas' life.

According to bystanders, Lencadio Sabala shot Banderas accidentally, and then fled, taking his gun with him. The witnesses claimed there had been no fight, no quarrel, but there had been drinking. They said Banderas and Sabala were sitting on beds on opposite sides of the tent they shared, facing each other. Sabala was playing with his revolver when it accidentally fired. This is where the rest of the story becomes somewhat suspicious, because then, onlookers said, Sabala was so upset, he *accidentally* pulled the trigger again. However, *three* wounds were found on Banderas' body: one in the left side of his chest, one in the left groin and the third through the left hand. When witnesses were presented with this 2 shots 3 wounds scenario, they claimed that two of the wounds must have been made by one bullet.

At the inquest those testifying were insistent the shooting was unintentional. One testified that Banderas, after he was shot, exclaimed, "You have shot me, but I forgive you." The jury, however, did not agree. To them it was murder. Yet all efforts to apprehend Sabala were futile. He escaped the long arm of the law.

The murder of another Mexican farm hand less than two weeks later had people scared. Was a murderous rampage taking place among Mexican laborers? Why weren't the police called immediately? Was anything being covered up?

On the evening of June 23, 1915, Francisco Morillo, foreman on the Grubert Brothers' sugar beet ranch at Los Alamitos, was shot and killed by his nephew, Carmilo Garcia. Like the Banderas case, the police were not notified of the killing until the next day. In this instance there were no witnesses. At the scene of the shooting police found a hat belonging to Garcia lying in a pool of blood. Three miles away they found a bloody handkerchief leading police to believe Garcia was seriously injured in the fight. A scabbard in which Morillo carried a knife was found empty. They believed the knife had ended up in Garcia's body.

The shooting occurred around 8:30 p.m. and was heard by Morillo's cousin Rosallo Lopez in a nearby bunk house. The scene police put together was this: Garcia and his uncle had been fighting, Morillo had bent down, possibly to pull his knife, and been killed while in a stooping position. According to friends the pair had been having disagreements over money, money which Garcia had borrowed from his uncle some time ago but not paid back. Fellow workers testified that Morillo told them he was going to Pete Labourdette's saloon to see his nephew *and* collect the money which had been promised him before the boy spent it all on drink. It is believed the pair met in the sugar beet fields and a fight began over the money which resulted in Morillo's death. Morillo was said to be a very resourceful man who saved his money for his family in Mexico. He had plans to return soon to Mexico. The 26-year-old Garcia was never found.

Many nationalities worked on the ranchos and farmland surrounding Long Beach. French, German, Italian, Spanish and even Hindi could be heard at shops, schools and churches in the area. It wasn't only Mexicans who had their share of misfortune. One tragedy involved two Swiss nationals.

Jacob Velier and Joseph Esalenta had come to America seeking their fortunes in Nevada mining. They made an unlikely pair, with Velier old enough to be Esalenta's father. But they were brought together by their common heritage; a heritage about which they argued constantly. After an unsuccessful attempt at mining they made their way to Long Beach and H.S. King's dairy farm, which was on land leased from the

Rancho Los Alamitos. Their disputes over Swiss politics, however, would lead to murder.

Esalenta was a Swiss from the Italian border while Velier was from the German side of Switzerland. The young 23-year-old Esalenta enjoyed arguing with 45-year-old Velier over Swiss history and was constantly seeking a quarrel with him, fellow workers testified. In one argument Esalenta told Velier that the country's hero, William Tell, who supposedly came from the German part of Switzerland, was just a legend. He had never existed. Upset that anyone could deny the existence of the country's greatest hero, Velier's temper exploded.

Ill feelings intensified the evening of July 15, 1908, and Velier drew a gun on Esalenta. Velier waved the gun around as he raged on over Esalenta's latest comments. As Velier moved closer to his verbal adversary, Esalenta spotted a bucket, picked it up and struck Velier on the head with it. Velier fired. The bullet struck Esalenta above the right eye, penetrating the skull and brain. He fell to the ground and died soon after.

Velier fled the scene but was soon captured. He did not appear alarmed over the murder, insisting he had only acted in self defense after repeated threats. The jury agreed.

Long Beach historian Loretta Berner had much to tell about one tragedy involving some Hindu ranchers. It was one she recounted in the *Los Fierros del Los Cerritos* magazine in 1967.

Loretta's mother was the cook at the Rancho Los Cerritos. It was up to her to appease the hunger of the many single men working on the rancho. She was a good chef, Loretta recounted, one who received many compliments from the hired hands she served. One evening as Loretta and her mother were washing the supper dishes, the dogs started barking. Loretta half expected the soft knock on the door to be from some hobo looking for a handout. Instead the two women were amazed to find a Hindu in native dress, one arm wrapped in a bloody sheet. Her mother's cry of terror brought farmhands to the kitchen. They recognized the man as Jojo, a local tenant farmer. While Loretta's mother tore clean sheeting into strips and bound up his wounded arm, the men tried to question him. His English was so poor all they could understand was "Laub shot me."

Nearly a year before the shooting three Hindus had rented a plot of ground near San Antonio Drive and Cherry Avenue. Some Japanese truck gardeners had left behind a makeshift house which the men moved into. They planted cabbages and in between work on their own place hired out as day laborers on nearby farms. No one ever knew the real names of two of them, they seemed to answer to Louie and Jojo, and these names stuck. They were friendly enough but usually kept to themselves, maybe because they spoke little English. Loretta remembered how fascinated she was watching Louie unroll his turban and refold it.

The third man, Laub Singh, was the spokesman of the group. Unlike the others he wore American style clothing, had short hair, and wore a fashionable hat, instead of a turban. His English was good and Loretta remembered he whistled as he rode a motorized bicycle around Long Beach and the rancho. In the middle of September 1918 Louie left, leaving Laub and Jojo to finish picking the last of the cabbage crop. It was then that Jojo was shot, ending up wounded in the rancho's kitchen. After getting the wound properly treated at a hospital Jojo returned to his home, and it seemed the two had patched up their differences. Then Laub disappeared, and a few days later Jojo was also gone.

The *Long Beach Press* of October 28, 1918, told the story: *"Gruesome Find Made by Hunter. Body of Mexican or Japanese discovered near Cerritos Slough."* The body was so badly decomposed that identification was not possible; it did appear, however, that the man had been murdered—there was a bullet hole in the right temple and his feet had been tied to his neck.

R.C. Andrews, the foreman on the Bixby Ranch identified the man as Laub Singh, a "Hindoo," who, along with two other Hindus, had rented farming land from the Bixbys. Andrews had recognized the body by the signet ring worn by the dead man. It was the same as the one worn by the missing tenant farmer.

According to Andrews, in September, one of the Hindus had come to the ranch house with a bloodied arm. All they could understand was "Laub shot me." After getting his wound dressed, the Hindu, Jojo, returned home, and the two seemed to have patched up their differences. Then Laub disappeared, and a few days later Jojo was also gone.

Authorities surmised Jojo killed Laub and carried the body to the slough. Since his feet were bound with a rope and his knees drawn up to his chin and the rope fastened around his neck, this seemed most likely. But how had Jojo, who had no car, transported the body over a mile from the camp which they occupied? Was the victim really Laub? Laub had a bike and knew how to ride it, Jojo didn't. The ring from the badly decomposed body could have been placed with the corpse to confuse police.

The murderer was never found, the theory being that Jojo had killed Laub and fled. Berner wrote that from that time on a whistle could be heard echoing through the denseness of the slough at midnight. Many believed the phantom whistle was the restless spirit of Laud, or was it really Jojo? In either case, the body of the victim was cremated, but his teeth were sent to India—an Indian custom. Perhaps the whistle was the Hindu, looking for his teeth.

Death in the Sugar Fields

Violence was almost commonplace among those who lived on the "outskirts of civilization" as some thought of the ranchos. Sometimes ranch hands wandered into downtown Long Beach and created quite a stir, which is what happened June 8, 1902. An inebriated Manuel Lopez had locals terrified as he waved his six-shooter at anyone he came across until he was finally arrested by Marshal Williams. Thrown in jail for the rest of the evening and fined $10 for his evening's amusement, he returned to the sugar beet fields the next day. Lopez learned the hard way that if you wanted a drink you didn't go to Long Beach. It was best to stay at Los Alamitos, surrounded by farms and fields and Pete Labourdette's saloon. The town of Los Alamitos was a rough and tough place to live and Labourdette's saloon would figure prominently in several murders, as the following story illustrates.

On the morning of April 14, 1903, the body of a young Mexican was found by a Pacific Electric work crew near Rancho Los Cerritos. His head was crushed and his throat cut from ear to ear. The corpse was fairly well dressed, but had nothing on him to make identification possible. Hundreds of persons gathered at the scene to view the body before the coroner arrived from Los Angeles, but none of them recognized the murdered man.

Police thought they had a clue when a motorman on the Long Beach electric line reported seeing a wagon the previous evening near where the body was later discovered. This, and the fact that there was little blood on the ground near the victim, led police to conclude the corpse was dumped at the Los Cerritos site. A pool of blood was found some distance away from the field where the wagon had been seen. Bloodhounds followed the scent for a while, but failed to find any evidence. The trail ended a quarter mile away on a road which wound along fences and through fields to the sugar factory at Los Alamitos. Police were convinced the murder had been committed in the fledgling town of Los Alamitos. There were several wineries in the sugar town and saloons of an unsavory nature. Two or three murders had been committed in or near Pete Labourdette's saloon and Labourdette had reason to fear his liquor license would be revoked if there was continued violence. Police surmised that the murder was committed in his saloon and the body moved to protect the saloonkeeper.

The rough and tumble town of Los Alamitos had sprung up around the local sugar beet factory. It had been Llewellyn Bixby who first saw the potential of sugar making in Southern California. Unable to finance a sugar factory himself, he persuaded William and James Clark to buy land, build the sugar factory at Los Alamitos and give the Bixbys preference when buying beets. As a result a large tract of Rancho Los Alamitos land was subdivided into ten and twenty acre ranches and rented to farmers with the stipulation that they plant certain crops. By December 1896 all 9,000 acres of land on the Alamitos Rancho was rented. Beets were planted on 3,600 acres and 5,000 acres devoted to corn and barley.

The Los Alamitos sugar beet factory opened Monday morning, July 21, 1897, at 6 a.m. For 100 days a continuous stream of beets, 12 tons per hour, entered the factory to have sugar extracted. The 1897 harvest season lasted from June 15th to October 25th. During that time 30,025 tons of sugar beets harvested from 2,887 acres were processed in the factory.

The owners of the sugar factory were to have a dramatic effect on the growth of Southern California. Montana Senator William A. Clark, nicknamed the "Montana Copper King," was said to be the largest individual owner of copper mines and smelters in the world; he was also considered one of the richest. Beginning with $1,500, earned by working the gold mines of Colorado and Montana, he became a Montana businessman and parlayed his money into a fortune. His younger brother, James, was also involved in various family enterprises. In 1892 James moved from Montana to Los Angeles and enthusiastically embraced the sugar beet possibilities Llewellyn Bixby envisioned.

In August 1896 sixty men began clearing land for the beet-sugar factory being built on former Rancho Los Alamitos property. The factory was set along a new rail line built by the Clark brothers connecting the factory with both Anaheim and Norwalk. In October 1896 a nine mile link of the rail line from Anaheim to the Los Alamitos Ranch was completed. There was a depot, telegraph line, hotel and Labourdette's saloon close to the factory. It was here the town of Los Alamitos began. Described by one reporter as resembling a mining camp, the town was raucous, rowdy and definitely alcohol friendly.

Less than a year after the sugar factory opened Labourdette was accused of murder. Daniel L. Ashby, a teamster driving his wagon from Compton to Los Alamitos in May 1898 supposedly fell asleep, lost his balance and ended up falling between the horses' feet. With his feet entangled in the reins he was dragged for more than a half-mile before dying. At the inquiry into the death it was noted that there was a wound on the right side of the head, and the skull was fractured. On the left side of the face and all along the left side of the body were abrasions and scratches. Footprints ten inches long were also discovered by the side of Ashby's wagon when his body was found. The only man known to have feet that big was Pete Labourdette. Had Labourdette killed the 50-year-old Ashby and then staged the accident? Labourdette did admit that Ashby had stopped at his saloon that evening, and that they had a few drinks together. Had a fight ensued and Ashby been killed? Though suspicions pointed to Labourdette as a murderer, nothing could be substantiated.

Labourdette saloon's savory reputation was often reported in the press. Arguments augmented by alcohol frequently resulted in fights. Disputes over gambling often erupted. In 1901 a Belgian laborer clubbed another Labourdette bar patron with a shotgun, inflicting an ugly dent near the right eye and cutting a big gash exposing the bone in the forehead. Even Labourdette was not immune to this violence. In March 1910 Trinidad Bravo stabbed Labourdette when Labourdette refused to serve him. Labourdette was not one to pick a fight with. He pursued Bravo, beating him brutally with a gun and club, breaking Bravo's arm, fracturing five ribs and cracking his skull.

Violence seemed almost common place in the beet fields surrounding the town of Los Alamitos. Fights often broke out among rival camps of beet cutters, their tempers fired up by Labourdette's alcohol. In September 1913 Long Beach police scoured the country around the sugar factory seeking Alegos Lopez and Jose Lemas wanted for the killing of Dolores Gonzales, who worked at another camp. Gonzales had died from a gunshot wound in the right groin, inflicted by Lopez in a knife and gun duel.

Sunday was not only a day of rest for many laboring in the beet fields: it was also a day of drink. On Sunday, September 21, 1913, the men of rival beet harvesting camps had ended the sacred day in a drunken brawl. Competition between the various work crews was intense. Who could harvest the beets quickest and make the most money? Who wielded the beet cutting knife fastest? Who was the most "macho?" Dolores Gonzales sported a black eye after such an argument with Alegos Lopez. In his alcohol driven rage Gonzales told Lopez the fight was not yet over. He would kill Alegos Lopez the first chance he got.

Even after sobering up Gonzales' anger consumed him. A few days later he confronted Alegos Lopez and Lopez's companion, Jose Lemas, on a lonely road near the sugar factory. He attacked them both with a beet knife. It was his ego driven belief that he could take on two men at once and regain his honor.

Lopez managed to avoid blows by deflecting them with a rifle he carried, but finally he could take no more. He opened fire. Lemas also fired at Gonzales with a revolver before Lemas and Lopez fled the scene. Gonzales fell, badly wounded; he lay weltering in his blood for nearly an hour before a passing rancher discovered him. However, it was too late; he had lost too much blood and after telling his story he died, believing he was the true victor. The cowardly Lopez and Lemas had not the courage to fight him with their knives, like men. They had to resort to their guns, two men against one. Gonzales may have believed he regained his honor, but Jose Lemas and Alegos Lopez escaped. Was honor enough to die for?

The beet cutters also fought, and died, over love. On July 3, 1916, Jose Ledesma lay dead with four deep stab wounds in his body. He had been attacked by J. Rodriquez who also lived on the De Ball ranch, two miles west of the sugar factory. They were both beet cutters, used to going to bed with their long machete-like beet cutting knives tucked under their pillows. Both were infatuated with the lovely daughter of De Ball's cook. Ledesma, however, seemed to be getting the lion's share of her smiles and Rodriguez was jealous. He challenged Ledesma; knives flashed in the dim light, there were cries, a heavy fall and groans. Ledesma, stabbed in four places, was dragged out of the bunk house dying while Rodriquez escaped.

A wedding, celebrated with plenty of alcohol, also brought forth a revengeful spirit consumed by unrequited love. On October 18, 1912, twenty-year-old Ramon Sandejas lay with two bullets in his body; Benito Dominguez and Andreas Ramos were in jail charged with the shooting. All were beet cutters who had just attended a friend's wedding.

Ramon Sandejas and Benito Dominguez were rivals for the same girl, who after flirting with both for several months finally decided she loved Sandejas the best. The jilted Dominguez didn't take his rejection well. At the wedding of their mutual friend, whisky and wine flowed freely and Sandejas and Dominguez, the alcohol consuming them, had several quarrels. However, friends broke things up before any serious trouble evolved.

At midnight, after the liquor had run low, Sandejas went to a winery to get more. Coming back he was met by a drunken Dominguez and Andreas Ramos. From the look on their faces and their slurred speech Sandejas knew that trouble couldn't be avoided this time. Realizing the odds were not in his favor, Ramon Sandejas pulled a knife to warn off the two men. Not to be bested, Dominguez drew a revolver and fired at Sandejas. One bullet entered Sandejas' chest above the heart and, glancing off a rib, came out under the left arm; another shot entered the right thigh from the rear, passing entirely through the leg. Sandejas fought back and was shot in the arm by Ramos.

But this story has a happy ending. Though murderous intent was in the air, Sandejas survived. He went on to marry the lovely senorita. Benito Dominguez and Andreas Ramos were sentenced to prison for assault.

Yet marriage didn't always mean living happily ever after, as a young wife soon found out.

Bernardino Castro worked hard cutting sugar beets. It was a job that often took him away from home for days at a time. Somehow he had found time to woo and win the heart of the loveliest senorita around. He didn't believe his luck, such a beautiful woman now his. But was she *all* his? As he worked in the fields he wondered what his wife was doing. He remembered her beautiful smile and the lustful looks of other men. Could she resist all this attention and avoid temptation?

On September 30, 1918, as Bernardino Castro was bringing a load of beets to the sugar factory he spotted his wife talking to another man. Consumed by jealousy the 22-year-old Castro pulled out his gun. Yelling obscenities he pulled the trigger, killing his wife instantly. He then turned his gun on the Mexican youth she was talking to. In Castro's mind his suspicions about her fidelity were confirmed.

Often police had no idea what had caused the melee they were investigating. Language differences contributed to the confusion, but sometimes they just never knew what had caused a fatal shooting. Such was the case of Pedro Escobar, an employee at the Los Alamitos sugar factory. On April 7, 1916, Pedro Escobar was shot by a fellow worker, Raquel Barras, following a quarrel. Witnesses refused to discuss what the argument had been all about.

Work in the sugar factory itself could be dangerous and deadly. Even dull jobs could bring death if one was not careful, as 17-year-old Clinton Coughran found out the evening of September 27, 1905. The teenager had been assigned the task of monitoring the dumping of sugar pulp into processing tanks. It was a routine boring job, especially at night when no one was around. Clinton was happy when two friends decided to visit during his lonely shift. Though it was against the rules, they decided that riding the electric trams which conveyed the pulp to a big tank outside the factory would be exciting and fun.

Once the cars dumped their pulp they were sent back empty. The teenagers decided to board the empty cars and ride them back into the factory. But all did not go as planned. Coughran had just dumped the pulp and was about to leap aboard the empty car when he missed his footing and was hurtled down into the tank. His horrified companions stopped the car and ran to his assistance. In the pulpy mash they found their dead friend, his head crushed and his body a sugary mass.

The Los Alamitos sugar factory was followed by four others in Orange County— in 1908 one was constructed on Main Street, just outside of Santa Ana; in 1911 another sprang up in Huntington Beach; and in 1912 two were built, one in Anaheim and the other on Dyer Road, south of Santa Ana.

The growth of the sugar beet industry had a profound effect on American life in the 20th century. The beet sugar provided an inexpensive alternative to cane sugar. New industries developed around this economical sugar product: cake mixes, jellies, preserves and other processed foods owe their existence to the development of beet sugars in America. By 1925, however, the soil of the Los Alamitos and Cerritos ranchos was depleted and no more beets would grow. Failure of many farmers to follow sound crop-rotation programs started the decline. Added to this was the trouble with pests and diseases which raged unchecked in the period immediately following World War I. And in the course of years, not just sugar beets, but all crops gradually had to make way for people. The Los Alamitos factory closed down and was eventually sold to Dr. Ross, a dog food maker. Later Los Alamitos race track was built on the site. Sugar beet processing remained in the area well into the 1950's, the last one being the Holly plant on Dyer road in Irvine. But it too, gave way to housing.

The Murderous Trolley

On February 3, 1902, one hundred men, most of them Mexicans from Long Beach's Sonoratown, began work on Henry Huntington's new Pacific Electric rail line running from Los Angeles to Long Beach. Sonoratown was a traveling Mexican village where thirty families working for the railroads and the Pacific Electric made their home. They lived in a dozen dingy freight cars, which traveled from work site to work site. At a moment's notice they would gather all their possessions, hastily pull up ladders and make a last grab for firewood before they were whisked away in their box car cottages to another part of the city. Theirs was a hard life; most of the rail cars were plain with crude furniture and a single "frijoles" pot. A few were more pretentious with a plant or two hung out of the small window. Every car, however, had a stove around which the family could huddle against the cold. Despite this frugal existence they knew how to have fun. At night you could hear the strains of music coming from a phonograph while the Mexican families cleared furniture from one of the box cars to dance. But the fun would soon stop as the tragedies of the electric road they were building enveloped them.

The new rail line was to be one of the fastest in the state. To accomplish this the men of Sonoratown had to put in four tracks instead of two, the extra ones used for non stop trains traveling from fifty to sixty miles an hour between Long Beach and Los Angeles. At first it seemed as if God didn't want this "fastest in the state" rail line built. Mrs. Carson, one of the daughters of the Dominguez family who still lived on the Dominguez rancho, was afraid the rumbling of the passing railway cars would cause the family's old chapel to crumble. Nothing the railroad people said could persuade her to let the trolley pass as close as their original route indicated. As a result, they had to change the course of the rail line, the new route passing over some early Native American sites. Trouble soon followed. On June 5th two cars on the new line collided head on. Fortunately no one was killed and Huntington was able to complete the tracks on time for the 4th of July celebrations in Long Beach.

By noon on the Fourth, a crowd of 30,000 men, women and children had poured into the city. Most came on the new trolley line, but a count showed 1,450 buggies and carriages parked along the beach. Fred Bixby from the Rancho Los Alamitos was there with one of the first automobiles in town, a "White Steamer." It attracted as much attention as Charles Drake's new bathhouse on the beach. In fact, there were so many people in town Drake decided to make as much money as he could and opened his new plunge, which still needed a roof built over the pool, that same red letter day.

With the exception of a twenty-minute interruption due to two supply systems getting out of step, the electric road was in steady operation throughout the day. The major problem for police was keeping the crowd off the tracks between the foot of Pine Avenue and the pier; fortunately there were no accidents. When night fell most visitors were exhausted. The town's hotels could not handle all the overnight guests. Several thousand people, too tired to take the trolleys back to Los Angeles, simply bedded down on the beach for the night.

Few participating in the events of July 4, 1902, were aware that it was an historic occasion, marking a turning point in Long Beach history. Prior to the arrival of the Red Car, as Huntington's red colored trolley was called, trains stopped in Long Beach twice a day; but the opening of the electric line with service every fifteen minutes dramatically altered the way of life in Long Beach. No longer was it a sleepy and isolated little seaside resort—quick, reliable transportation pummeled the town into an age of tremendous growth and prosperity. By the 1910 U.S. census, Long Beach had grown eightfold, from a population of around 2,000 in 1900 to one of 17,809. It was promoted as the fastest growing city in the United States—all this growth taking place because of the Pacific Electric.

But all of this was not without cost. It seemed the Red Car, or perhaps the spirits of those Native Americans over whose ground the rail line traveled, had a grudge to settle with those who built it. On July 19, 1902, two weeks after the new Long Beach electric line opened, a Mexican worker was killed. The unidentified victim had been on the tracks when he was struck by a Red Car carrying a work crew. In his pockets were $9.40 and a brass tag of the electric company, numbered 447. Aside from a bad gash on the back of the right hand and a long bruise on the right side of the head, the body showed few marks. It was assumed he died of internal injuries.

The second fatal accident on the new electric line also resulted in the death of another unidentified Mexican worker. The car, bound from Long Beach to Los Angeles, was traveling at about 40 miles an hour. As it neared Compton the motorman saw a man working on the track. Though the bell of the car was rung, the man seemed to pay no attention to it. He was either deaf or his mind had wandered off somewhere. The car managed to stop, but the man, who carried no identity papers with him, staggered into the car which he apparently did not see. He was knocked clear of the track. When help reached him he was scarcely breathing. He died aboard the electric car before he could reach a hospital.

Death became the master of ceremonies on July 4, 1903, the first anniversary of the Red Car's arrival in Long Beach. Three lives were sacrificed to the demon train. All were individual accidents, in no way related to each other except for one factor: all were killed by a speeding electric train.

Gregorio Encinal, who had worked for Jotham Bixby since 1884, was surprised to see Mr. Bixby driving up the road toward the Encinal house late on the evening of July 4th. It was unusual for Mr. Bixby to come at dusk and all were a bit apprehensive. When they saw Bixby's weathered grim face they knew for sure that something was wrong. Bixby took Gregorio aside and told them that there had been an accident. Then he broke the sad news as gently as possible. Esiquio, Gregorio's brother who had a beet farm in what is now North Long Beach, was dead.

Esiquio had been looking forward to the Fourth of July celebrations in Long Beach. He had worked hard to get the farm in order and allow himself time off. Since the Pacific Electric line ran right past his farm all Esiquio had to do was signal for a car bound for Long Beach to stop. As an oncoming car approached Esiquio waved, but thinking the motorman did not see him, he stepped across the track to one on which another car was coming. Although the motorman rang the bell vigorously, Encinal didn't move fast enough. He was hit and killed. He was caught between two of the new Pacific Electric cars and crushed to death.

The second victim was also a Mexican, unidentified, and his death was due to falling from an overcrowded car.

The third accident happened before the eyes of Frank Springer's parents as they were sitting in front of their home at Eleventh Street and American Avenue in Long Beach, waiting for their son to return from a trip to the beach. Twenty-one-year-old Frank had been to the pavilion enjoying the dancing and other Fourth of July activities. Usually, Frank got off the electric car as it passed his house. However, this holiday evening the car was so crowded Springer was forced to stand in the aisle. When the train slowed down near his home he found it easier to get off on the side next to the other track instead of on the safer side toward the roadway. When he jumped from the car he failed to notice another car whizzing along from Los Angeles. Before he could recover his balance and leap out of the way, the car struck him, hurling him many feet and killing him instantly.

These three deaths all happened on the first anniversary of the Pacific Electric's arrival in Long Beach. In its first year of service Esiquio Encinal, Jacinto Chavez, Milton LaFetra, Frank Springer, Thomas Smiley and three unidentified Mexicans had all lost their lives to the electric train that was bringing so much prosperity to Long Beach. Perhaps the most poignant death of all was that of Louisa Pardo. The young Mexican mother had given her life in order to save her six-year-old son who was playing on the rail line.

The murderous trolley would continue to kill. Hundreds more would lose their lives on the tracks of the Pacific Electric until the trolley itself came to a slow death in 1961. But not all the deaths took place outside the cars.

A battered, blood-stained Santa Monica Red Car pulled in at Los Angeles the night of August 27, 1906, with the limp body of a murdered woman lying in a pool of bloody gore between the seats. The hideous murder of Jennie Cook had occurred as the electric car sped along its route, the woman shot to death by a man riding in the seat next to her. After a fearful fight with another passenger the killer broke away, ran back through the car, past the conductor, and jumped off into the night. Though the electric car stopped, no trace of the murderer could be found. Hoping to get more help as quickly as possible, the conductor sent the car off at record speed into Los Angeles. Stunned and not knowing what to do with the dead body, the conductor told passengers to leave the victim in her seat. But the high speed of the train caused the body to slip down until at last the corpse fell between the seats; only the pathetic, shabby little shoes stuck out into the aisle to haunt those who made the terrible ride, the *Los Angeles Times* reported.

It seemed that Jennie Cook had a premonition that something was going to happen. Her ex-husband Fred had been following her and threatening to kill her unless she gave him their son or returned to live with him. She told people at the detention home where she worked that she feared her ex-husband might get on the same trolley car with her some day. However, she said she had a plan to lose him: she'd jump off the train and run. Unhappily for her she didn't get a chance to execute her plan of action.

Fred was often seen hanging around the detention home in hopes of meeting Jennie. She had left him before their baby was born three years earlier. It seemed Fred was a believer in free love and had found another partner with whom he could practice his new religion. Helpless and destitute, Jennie had at last found employment at the detention home where she also lived. It seemed a safe place to live with others around to watch out for her. However, Fred was desperate to have her back. He had once climbed a ladder and tried to get into her room before guards chased him away. Jennie thought it best to leave her son with a relative and had been coming back from visiting him when Fred confronted her. It appeared that cold-blooded planning preceded the murder. Cook had dyed his hair red, bought a false moustache and new clothes. Thus disguised, he was able to approach his victim.

Witnesses said there was nothing unusual in the conduct of the couple who had gotten on the train together. They thought it somewhat odd, but not uncommon, that the man had gotten up and asked the woman to change seats with him so he could sit on the aisle side. She had agreed. It was a decision that would cost Jennie her life. Had she recognized her ex-husband in his disguise? Little did she suspect he had asked to change seats so he could more easily shoot her. Without getting up, and without a word, Cook pulled a revolver and fired into his ex-wife's forehead. Stunned passengers reported he sprang to his feet and fired twice more. It was all so quick that the second shot had already been fired before anyone noticed anything unusual.

L.P. Bishop, sitting behind Cook, jumped up and tried to get the gun away from the murderer. They struggled and Cook shot at him, but the bullet went wild and Bishop knocked the pistol from Cook's hand. As they struggled they went crashing through the heavy plate-glass front window of the car, raining glass everywhere. Somehow Cook managed to escape, jumping off the back platform while the car was going over twenty miles an hour.

Cook was spotted in Long Beach, Tujunga Canyon and several other places before he was finally captured. Ironically it was his wife's devotion to him that led to her murder. It seemed that many thought Cook insane. It appeared to run in his family and it was only through Jennie Cook's intercession that Cook hadn't been incarcerated in the Westborough Insane Asylum in Massachusetts.

On April 23, 1908, Cook was sentenced to life imprisonment for the murder of his wife. On the way to prison Cook was in a dazed condition, reciting fairy stories to himself.

Murderous Sea

In the days before air conditioning scores of inlanders would escape the stifling heat by spending their summers at the beach. Many would rent cottages by the sea, but even more would simply pitch a tent along the sand and enjoy the cool sea breeze and camping lifestyle. These dream cities of summer were a west coast phenomena. Along the Atlantic coast these "tent cities" as they were called were unknown. Thunder storms, windy weather and hurricanes made them impossible, but on the Pacific coast people could live under canvas the year round. The novelty of these communities attracted people from all over the United States and Europe to the tent cities of Coronado, Avalon and Long Beach. There were at least six thousand people tenting it along Southern California beaches in July 1901. "To see the coast from a balloon it would seem as if the camps of an army were pitched upon our shores," the *Los Angeles Times* reported (June 14, 1901). Three months was the usual length of life of these seaside tent cities. By the first of July they would be in full swing; the last of September they would have disappeared seemingly into the sand itself.

In Long Beach that summer of 1901 fifty tents were pitched on the sand, and fifty more back in a grove of eucalyptus trees. Here the camper would find a butcher, baker, milkman, grocer and vegetable vendor walking through the tent city each day offering their products for sale. Good drinking water was provided to the camper free of charge; refuse was hauled away and the streets cleaned every morning. A fully furnished tent rented for about $18 per month. Summer sojourners could also bring their own tent and furniture and rent vacant lots for about four dollars a month. Those from the sweltering Riverside area came in specially constructed wagons in which they camped for the whole season. They were as comfortable as any tent and formed a picturesque section of the beach village.

These summer communities were laid out on regular streets, like any town, and miles of plank sidewalks led from the canvas homes pitched on the beach. Each had its own individual style. In some an additional room or pantry had been made by adding a piano box to the rear; in another an extra room made of cheese cloth had been attached. Long fishing poles leaned against the walls of some, while gasoline stoves and extra cots could be seen lining the front of others. It was a free, neighborly life. The stiff proprieties that people held in regular city living could not exist in a place where you saw and heard your neighbor going to bed every night and getting up in the morning.

In 1932 Ella Howard shared memories of 1901 Long Beach with Walter Case's *Did You Know That?* readers. She remembered coming to Long Beach by train, passing acres and acres of barley fields. It was a crop that would grow without irrigation, so was a favorite commodity for farmers. At the rail station she saw campers with baggage of all shapes and sizes, rolled tents, household utensils tied up in blankets, handbags, market baskets, all brought by the railroad and dumped in a heap at the station. Howard, here to give demonstrations in domestic science at the Chautauqua, stayed at the Butler Hotel on Ocean Boulevard. It was so noisy with the campers on the beach, horses and buggies and horse-drawn trucks rattling by on the street that she had a hard time sleeping. Mosquitoes were the biggest problem, especially when the wind blew over the salt marshes, bringing the troublesome insects closer to town. The flying pests were so bad that horses wore netting over their ears and faces and workmen wore broad straw hats covered with netting drawn in and tied at the neck. Large quantities of crude oil poured on the marshes helped matters, but then there was the sand. Sand was everywhere. Despite the mosquitoes and sand, six thousand or more people came for the two week Chautauqua lectures which opened after the Fourth of July. Many stayed on for the four week Methodist camp meeting and Christian Church convention which followed.

Among those staying in Long Beach's tent city that summer of 1901 was the Wallace family from Los Angeles. There was plenty to keep them busy. For food all they needed was a fishing rod to get fresh fish, and a shovel at low tide to bring up clams. For entertainment there was the Pine Avenue Pier to stroll on and the various lectures held at the Chautauqua and Methodist conventions. During the day they basked in the sun and swam in the surf. By night they dodged mosquitoes and watched the star filled sky, wishing on the falling stars so prevalent during the annual August Leonid meteor showers. But they were soon to discover that all their wishing could not bring back the lives of their two daughters and niece. They had learned the hard way that the ocean could be a murderous place, especially for those who could not swim.

For fifteen August days all of Southern California shared the anguish of Mr. & Mrs. Sam Wallace as they awaited news of their daughter Elsie. Fifteen-year-old Imogene, eighteen-year-old Elsie and twenty-year-old Cora Wallace were last seen alive August 10, 1901, bathing off the Pine Avenue Pier. They were with Fred Wilkinson and Harry Smith when an incoming wave swept all five off their feet. Onlookers saw the girls and young men struggle with an undertow and pulled under before help could reach them. Smith was carried away from the others, but Wilkinson briefly held one of the girls by her hand while the other two also linked hands. But the pull of the waves broke their hold. None of the young women knew how to swim, though Elsie had been taking lessons. Smith and Wilkinson eventually made it to shore, but the three girls could not be seen.

A short time later Cora Wallace's body was washed ashore, about 200 feet east from where they had disappeared in the sea. For two hours attempts were made to resuscitate her while beachgoers searched the surf for the other young women, but to no avail. Cora Wallace died. Her body was returned to the tent of her aunt and uncle, while searchers were still striving to recover the remains of their daughters.

Twelve days later, on August 22, 1901, fishermen found a body washed up on the sand. Though it was so badly decomposed and the face disfigured almost beyond recognition, the clothing identified the victim as Imogene Wallace. No formal identification was made by the parents "for fear the memory of seeing it (according to the *Evening Tribune*) would haunt them forever." The paper added:

"Friends of the family describe the agony of the parents during these awful days as most heartrending. Day after day have they silently paced up and down the seashore, watching and hoping the waves would give up their treasures. In all the weary waiting no ray of comfort has come to them, and still they must wait, for the other daughter is still missing. God help the doubly bereaved parents." (*Evening Tribune* 8/22/1901)

Elsie's remains were discovered August 25th, the day of Cora and Imogene's funeral. Fishermen on the Pine Avenue Pier saw a dark body tossing on the water not far from where the old Magnolia Avenue Pier used to stand. A boat was sent to investigate, and it proved to be the long-sought-for body of Elsie Wallace. Wrapping it in canvas the crew brought it back to shore, where it was immediately taken to Wilson's

Undertaking Parlors. It was thought that Elsie's body had become entangled in the seaweed around the old Magnolia Pier because her hair was thickly matted with kelp. Cora and Imogene's funeral was postponed until Elsie joined them the following day.

On Sunday, August 26, 1901, three white caskets covered with white roses lay side by side. Three hearts of white carnations and roses were interlinked, as the girls were taken off for burial in Evergreen Cemetery in Los Angeles.

Long Beach officials were quick to point out that these were the first deaths by drowning since 1896 when Grafton Abernathy, who was consumptive, drowned after spending too much time in the water. There had been a couple drownings since then but none of them had been swimmers, or dressed in bathing clothes. All in all, Long Beach was a safe place to bathe, officials told the press. But they were wrong.

On June 27, 1902, two strong men, J. Howard Long and E. Hayslip died in separate drownings off the shore in Long Beach. Huge waves and a strong rip tide that could be seen like a river flowing out through the sea greeted swimmers that day. The men should have known how to deal with the conditions, but they didn't. Hayslip's body was recovered that day, Long's four days later. Less than three weeks later two other men, Elmer Blum and Hjalmar Sundberg, lost their lives to the sea. All four drownings had taken place in front of Tent City. City officials said it would be impossible for lifeguards to patrol the nearly ten miles of beach which gave Long Beach its name. But something had to be done, and it would be done by Charles Drake, owner of the fledgling amusement zone that would become known as the Pike.

In May 1901 Arizona millionaire Charles Drake bought the holdings of the Long Beach Development Company, Boulton Water Company and parts of the Banning Company. His new company, called the Seaside Water Company, purchased beach front land to build an amusement area. Later in 1901 Drake successfully obtained the Long Beach electric railway franchise for his friend Henry Huntington. Drake knew the electric railway would bring many more tourists into the city and his amusement park would profit.

On February 5, 1902, Drake broke ground for his first venture into the tourist business—a bathhouse on the beach. Now the drownings and bad publicity had him worried. Long Beach officials had publicly stated the city could not be expected to patrol its entire beach front. Drake realized that unless some measures were taken to reduce the public's concern about the rip tides and drownings in Long Beach his new amusement zone could lose money. He quickly promised to put in lines and floats and establish a lifesaving patrol in front of his bathhouse. Two men were hired to patrol the beach and a dory readied for rescue.

Long Beach city officials finally admitted they too needed to do something. Signs were posted warning of the dangerous rip tides and a big raft anchored outside the breakers in front of Tent City.

Sometimes the sea would be blamed for acts it did not wantonly commit.

There was nothing on the drowning victim to help with identification except some papers with the name of N. Castello written on them. The corpse's pockets were filled with sand, a cheap watch, a $5 gold piece and $2.35 in silver. He was found without a coat, but a coat was found on the sand near the body which matched his vest and trousers. Officials were at a loss to explain how the coat could have been removed. Coroner Holland suggested the victim might have thrown his arms back and the outer garment dropped off or was washed off by the action of the water. The inquest disclosed nothing that would lead to his identity, except the name N. Castello written on the scraps of paper.

The victim was described as being 5 feet 10 inches in height, weighting 175 pounds. The body was in a bad state of decomposition, the flesh having nearly all fallen from face, hands and feet. The remains were laid away in potter's field at the Municipal Cemetery.

Several people came forward after the description appeared in local newspapers. F.X. Palmer thought the unidentified man could have been real estate agent J.N. Castello whose description resembled the dead man's. Palmer believed Castello had taken a steamship from San Francisco to San Pedro and somehow met an accident along the way. But the truth to the identity of the drowning victim lay in the Long Beach post office. A letter and package was found addressed to Nicholas J. Castello in care of general delivery. By tracing the mail back to Mrs. Mary Stevenson, one of Castello's sisters, authorities were able to confirm the dead man's identity.

Castello, it was learned, came to Long Beach on December 13, 1903, intending to remain three weeks. The question as to whether his death was suicide or an accident remained undetermined. It appeared, however, the 32-year-old bachelor was well to do. By profession he was a druggist with $2,700 on deposit in a bank in San Francisco. His body was disinterred and sent by Wells Fargo and Company to his sisters in San Francisco.

But was it really Nicholas Castello? His body was so badly decomposed that identification was almost impossible. The scrap of paper could have been planted, as well as the letter and package in the post office. Then there was the suspicious nature of his coat being removed from his body, and being found some distance away. Could Nicholas Castello have taken advantage of a poor drowning victim and staged his own disappearance? Could he have arranged the death?

It was almost impossible to stage a fake drowning in Long Beach, as an article in the October 31, 1904, *Evening Tribune* pointed out. The headline read: *Sea Gives Up Its Dead: Remarkable Fact Regarding Long Beach Bay. Sooner of Later Bodies Will Rise to Surface*:

"In the history of our city there has never been a disappearance that has not been accounted for either by the finding of the body or the apprehension of a fugitive from justice. As a rule the corpse rises to the surface in 7 or 10 days, though in one instance, it was fifteen. In the past year there have been four fake drownings."

In one instance Warren T. Coolidge, out walking with two companions on the outer end of the wharf, was reported to have stumbled while reaching for his hat. He fell into twenty-five feet of water. His hat was recovered but no trace of the body was found. His life was heavily insured, and he was later found in Wyoming. A few months later bathhouse employees found a suit of clothing, shoes and stockings in a bathroom and in a safety box found a watch and address of J.F. Schufflebarger. Bad debts had forced him to fake his death. He was later discovered in Arizona. But had Nicholas Castello been an exception?

Another drowning victim was buried in potter's field in 1903. Twenty-eight-year- old G.T. Morris of Terminal Island was found in a little slough draining into the ocean on the afternoon of April 22, 1903. He had been having difficulty paying his rent and when Marshal Tom Williams called at his house Morris ran away. Williams fired twice in the air to frighten him. Morris didn't stop but continued to lead the marshal a merry chase over the flats west of town. The coroner believed Morris, distressed over his troubles, committed suicide by drowning, though there was the rumor the marshal had accidentally shot Morris and should be tried for murder. The coroner, however, found no reason to doubt that Morris had drowned, but he ruled it an accident, not suicide. Since Morris' wife, who had left him the previous week, could not be found, the body was quickly buried in potter's field at the Municipal Cemetery on Signal Hill.

On September 13, 1908, Emmett Cochran, who claimed to be a miner from Barstow, went swimming in the Long Beach surf and, judging from all appearances, drowned. His clothes were in the bathhouse, locked where he left them, and his valuables were still in the bathhouse safe. No one saw him go down, not even the lifeguards patrolling the beach, and no body was found.

Events got even more peculiar when his probable widow arrived in town. She told officials her husband had $800 in a money belt when he left home, yet no money belt was found among his possessions. Another curious fact was that he had just taken out an accident policy for $7,000. The mystery deepened when the U.S. Secret Service arrived in Long Beach and began their own investigation into Cochran's disappearance. Though the Secret Service was closed mouthed about their interest in the matter, rumor had it that Emmett Cochran was a member of a gang involved in smuggling Chinese and opium into the country and that the Secret Service was on his trail. Events pointed to the fact that Cochran knew they were closing in on him and he had staged his own disappearance.

Emmett Cochran did surface again, in July 1909, this time in Chicago under the name of Bert Scott. It appeared that Cochran, a former Secret Service agent, disappeared in Long Beach while en route to Mexico to invest funds in mining operations for a group of businessmen. The Northern California investment group was convinced Cochran had drowned and tried to collect $5,000 from two life insurance policies he had taken out just before he left for Mexico. The insurance companies, however, were not so sure of his death and sent Pinkerton agents to follow his trail. In Mexico they found enough evidence to convince them he was alive and somewhere in Argentina. They traced Cochran to Buenos Aires, where they found he was involved in counterfeiting, and back to Illinois. Still followed by Pinkerton agents, Cochran was arrested and sentenced to three years in the federal penitentiary at Leavenworth. His wife filed for divorce when a picture of another woman was found in his possession.

Sometimes the sea became the unsuspecting recipient of a body. On September 28, 1911, sailors on the steamer *Nellie*, returning from Catalina, found the body of an aged man floating in the water. The corpse appeared to have been in the ocean for about two weeks. The skull had been fractured by a severe blow behind the right ear, obviously before the body entered the water, and there was a gaping gash on the left side of the neck, which seemed to have been inflicted by a right-handed assassin. There was some question as to the identity of the body. Some said it couldn't be 82-year-old S. J. Buchanon, who had been missing for almost two weeks; the teeth of the corpse were too good for someone that age. However the faded laundry marks on the dead man's socks were deciphered and pointed to Buchanon. But anyone could have switched socks with the man. Finally George Lipscomb, who had known knew Buchanon for 40 years, examined the body and identified it by means of a deformed ear and short forefinger.

S.J. Buchanon, a wealthy miner from Montana, had retired to Long Beach to escape the frigid winter weather and enjoy the warm climate of Southern California. He was an amicable bachelor, very fond of strolling about the beach. He always had plenty of money and generally carried about $600 in his pockets, friends recounted. The Montana miner mysteriously disappeared from his apartment house around September 15th. Because of his love for the ocean some believed he had walked out on the jetties and fallen into the water, cracking his skull. Authorities, however, noticed a deep wound on the left side of his neck which could have been inflicted by a knife. Yet the body was so badly decomposed it was hard to tell. No money was found on the man, so robbery could have been a motive behind murder. A coroner's jury decided Buchanon's death came by a blow on the head, the cause of which was unknown.

Lucky Lady, Dead Husband

There were only 21 African Americans living in Long Beach during the time of the 1900 U.S. Census. The city at that time boasted a population of 2, 252; and 95.8% was white. Most African Americans were cooks, housekeepers, farm workers or hotel employees. There was the Andrew Parker family who rented a house on Elm. Andrew worked as a laundryman and supported his sister-in-law and niece, as well as his wife and daughter. Edward Russel owned his own dairy farm on Atlantic where he lived with his French Canadian wife and two children. John Sylver was a black man from Portugal who rented land from George Bixby. A few years earlier there would have been several more African Americans living in Long Beach, but on August 16, 1897, George Waters, crazed by jealousy and upset over losing his job, shot a hole in his wife's face and sent a bullet into his own brain.

Fifty-year-old Waters, employed as a coachman for Dr. J.T. Stewart, was described as quiet, courteous, hard working and industrious. Waters lived at the Stewart home while his wife and two children rented rooms at the Porter residence on Locust Street in downtown Long Beach. On weekends Waters visited. It was difficult being away from his family most of the week, but finding a good job was hard. Little did Waters suspect how tough times would become. Because of financial difficulties Stewart had to let Waters go.

Besides losing his job, Waters suspected his wife was having an affair. He confronted and accused her of "undue intimacy" with another man, a cook at the Henderson Hotel. Mrs. Waters denied the affair, but the two quarreled violently. Mrs. Waters, who knew her husband had a gun, was afraid he might use it. She and her two children slipped away from their home and spent the night following the confrontation at the Henderson Hotel, the only local hotel that would allow African Americans.

Fearing for her life, Mrs. Waters asked the police to issue a warrant for her husband's arrest. She was doubly fearful that by staying at the Henderson her husband might think she had fled to the arms of her supposed lover. But the police refused, thinking Mrs. Waters was exaggerating matters. To appease her they sent an officer to talk to Waters. Waters told police it had simply been a domestic dispute, but he promised to behave himself in the future. He lied.

Angry at his wife for sending the police after him, he returned home and the quarrel was renewed with even greater fury than before. Neighbors heard loud and angry words shouted through the walls, followed by pistol fire. A few moments later the door was thrown open and Mrs. Waters rushed out holding her hands to her face and screaming "I am shot." Waters followed and fired a second shot, which crashed through a window. Then, returning to the kitchen, he placed the gun to his head and pulled the trigger. The bullet entered his right cheekbone, traveled upward, severing the muscles and nerves of the right eye and eventually lodged in the brain. George Waters fell to the floor unconscious. The press described a ghastly scene: Waters lying like a log on the blood-bespattered floor with his right eye hanging on his cheek and black gore oozing from a ragged hole in his face (*LA Times* 8/17/1897). He died the next day.

This was almost Long Beach's second case of murder-suicide, following that of Mabel Myers in 1895. But in this case the fortunate victim lived. Mrs. Waters, though in great pain, suffered no permanent injury.

Shamed To Death

The Julian Hotel desk clerk didn't know what to do. The Long Beach hostelry prided itself on fine service from a quality staff, now one of their guests was complaining of not feeling well. Earlier she had been in the hotel dining room. Had their guest, Mary Black, eaten something that didn't agree with her? Her moaning and groaning was beginning to frighten the staff, but she wouldn't allow them to call in a doctor. Finally the hotel manager took matters into his own hands and summoned Dr. Welbourn.

Mrs. Black refused to tell the doctor what troubled her, but she did assure him her pain wasn't due to food poisoning. All she did say was that she was very worried. Unable to help her because of her refusal to allow an examination, the doctor left. Dr. Welbourn did, however, tell the manager to check in on her every hour or so and if she got worse call him. Hotel staff followed the doctor's orders, but when they next checked on Mary Black they found their guest lying on the floor, nearly nude and frothing at the mouth. She died an hour later. An autopsy revealed she had taken poison.

The investigation into the death of Mary Black in March 1899 brought out a shocking story of shame and wrong against her absent husband and children. It also cast an unfavorable shadow over the man who claimed to love her. Who was this woman who had taken her own life? Los Angeles neighbors of Mrs. Black said she had arrived in Southern California in December 1898. She seemed well to do and received money regularly from England. She had a frequent visitor, Gerard Mitchell, an Englishman who told the coroner he had recently arrived in Los Angeles and had no job, but he and Mrs. Black were to be married. They were just waiting for the death of her husband, who was in poor health.

The story Mitchell told sounded like something out of a Victorian romance novel. He was the son of a poor clergyman who had left England to seek his fortune in America. Fate led him to Fred Schultze's ranch in San Antonio, Texas, where he met Fred's sister, Mary. Mary, known as Nellie to her friends, had left her husband and two children in England. Married at the age of 17 to an ogre of a man, Mary finally convinced him to let her visit her brother in Texas. She refused to go back, telling her husband that her heart disease prevented her from traveling. Common interests drew 36-year-old Gerard and 43-year-old Mary together. They fell deeply in love. Divorce was unthinkable since neither Mary nor Mitchell had any money of their own, and it would bring shame to both families. Mitchell left for a job in Mexico, but love finally won out. The following year the couple agreed to meet in Los Angeles. In December 1898 they came to Los Angeles separately, Mary traveling from Texas, Mitchell from Mexico. Here they lived together as man and wife, with Mary's estranged husband, knowing nothing of her affair with Mitchell, sending her money to live on.

But shame over their adulterous actions tormented Mary and Gerard. The religious convictions they had been brought up believing in weighed heavily on their souls. Guilt finally caught up with them.

Somehow Mary's brother heard of their living arrangement and he pleaded with them to live separately for propriety's sake. He told them that Mary's husband was ill. It was only a matter of time before Martin

Black died and Gerard and Mary could legally marry. Mary was torn. What should she do? Should she return to her husband's bedside and be with him at the end? She hadn't seen him for nine years. What would happen to her two children once her husband died? But Mary knew she didn't have the strength to face her past.

Mary and Gerard decided to take things one step at a time. Though Mary told Gerard it would be the death of her to leave him, they agreed it would be better for appearance sake for them to live alone for awhile. Mary left the house the two had purchased together and took rooms in a nearby boarding house. Gerard said he knew nothing about the events leading up to Mary's supposed suicide, but thought it was because someone had found out about their past living arrangement and she could not live with the shame.

Two days after Mary's death Gerard went to the house he owned with Mary and ingested both strychnine and laudanum. He also slashed his wrists with a razor and cut his throat. His body was discovered by a woman looking to buy the home. Mitchell was still conscious, but he couldn't talk because of his severed windpipe. The bloody razor was found lying on the pillow and the razor case was on a chair by the bed. The bottle of laudanum and a paper containing strychnine were found on a chair in the corner of the bedroom. He died an hour later.

Why had Gerard committed suicide? Without Mary he was penniless. He had spent all his money in buying furniture for the house and paying for medical treatments for himself. Was this lack of money the cause of his death, or was it truly a desire to be with the woman he loved?

Circumstance, or fate, brought the two together once again. The remains of both were sent to Evergreen Cemetery in Los Angeles and, coincidently, buried side by side.

Cycling to Death

On July 25, 1899, 25-year-old Dorothy McKee and her friend, Anna Scudder, arose at 6 a.m. to pursue the latest sporting craze— cycling. During the decade of the 1890's some 10 million Americans took to the wheel, including Dorothy McKee. Though some, such as the Woman's Rescue League, led a national crusade against the use of the bicycle by women because it was immodest and offered "evil associations and opportunities," *(LA Times 7/2/1896)* Dorothy followed the rules of wheel etiquette outlined in *"A Wheel Woman's Manual."*

The first rule an up-to-date young woman had to understand was that the word "cycling" was the correct term; young women should not speak of bicycling or of wheeling. The same rules of etiquette that applied to driving a carriage also applied to cycling. The early morning hours, before noon, were acceptable. Afternoon hours were not. Nor was it correct for a young woman to ride unaccompanied; unmarried women should be chaperoned by a married lady, male escort, maid or groom. Dorothy was following all the rules. She was cycling with a married friend, before noon.

It was a beautiful morning and the tide on the beach was low, which provided an excellent cycling path miles in length. The two women were enjoying their ride and were well west of Long Beach and returning eastward when they met Dorothy's neighbor, Edward Methever, cycling toward them. The proper etiquette would have been for the 55-year-old Methever to stop and talk to the young ladies. However, he did no such thing. He rode straight at Dorothy forcing them to crash into each other.

There was a strange look in Methever's eyes, Anna Scudder later admitted, a peculiar determination in the way he directed himself towards Dorothy forcing them to collide. Anna just cycled on, thinking it a minor mishap, but soon she heard a shot. She turned and saw Methever firing a revolver rapidly at Dorothy McKee. Mrs. Scudder thought Methever was just joking around with a toy pistol, but didn't realize it was real until she saw blood flowing from Dorothy's wounds.

Three shots had been fired at the young woman as she fell from her bicycle in front of Tent City. Though one shot missed, one bullet entered the left side of her chin and emerged through the right ear, cutting the lobe. The other bullet entered high on the left breast and came out low down at the right of the back. Doctors later testified that death was due to internal hemorrhaging and could have been caused by either shot. After firing at Dorothy, Methever turned the gun on himself. The bullet entered in front of his right ear and emerged through his right eye. But it did not kill him. As Methever reached for another gun, a bystander rushed in and grabbed the weapon right before Methever collapsed. Some claimed Methever smelled of alcohol.

What had caused Methever, who was nearly 30 years older than Dorothy, to act in such a way? Most believed it was a case of unwarranted jealousy. Dorothy and her mother owned a bakery store on Pine Avenue. The other half of the building was occupied by Methever, who kept a small shoe store and cobbler's establishment. Dorothy and Methever were friendly and Dorothy, who viewed Methever as nothing more than a friend, went fishing with him a few times. There was never any romantic entanglement, at least on her part, and Methever never mentioned marriage or anything along those lines to Dorothy. That would have been improper, especially since Methever was already married, having deserted his wife and two children.

Dorothy and Anna Scudder were avid cyclists. They had gone cycling the day before the shooting with a young man, Isaac Baker. Later that evening Dorothy brought Isaac home, where they discussed their engagement and future plans. Mrs. Scudder was sure Methever, who she had heard coughing through the walls, overheard the conversation. Anna Scudder surmised that Methever must have become jealous, opened the whiskey bottle, and in a fit of drunken anger got on his bicycle the next morning to pursue and shoot Dorothy.

At his trial Methever testified to being very ill four months before the shooting. In order to alleviate the sharp pains in his head, he said he drank a pint or more of whisky every night. The drinking continued until the pain subsided. The night before the murder he had again had a return of the grippe, and the trouble with his head got worse. He remembered hearing people talking about him outside his window. Scared, he got his gun; after that didn't remember anything, including shooting Dorothy. His next memory was waking in the hospital the day after the shooting. He had no recollection of hearing Dorothy's conversation with Isaac. He also swore he had not taken a drink that night.

Edward Methever also gave details about his past, which could have led to this lapse of memory. Born in Vermont, he worked on a steamboat just prior to the Civil War. On the ship he was accidentally struck on the head with a crowbar, knocked senseless and confined in a hospital for two months. While serving in the army at New Orleans, he came down with what was called "black swamp" fever, and was laid up three or four months. After leaving the army he became a shoemaker. But more accidents followed. While moving from one town in Missouri to another, he was again knocked unconscious by a fence rail striking him on the head. He couldn't work for two months. Later, while learning to ride a bicycle, the handle bars loosened and he fell, again injuring his head. Though the defense claimed Methever was suffering from "delirium tremens" and was not mentally capable of knowing what he was doing, Methever was found guilty of murder in the first degree.

Up to the end Methever proclaimed his innocence. On March 28, 1901, *Los Angeles Times* reporters were granted a final interview with the man condemned to death. Methever maintained he and Dorothy were just good friends, he wasn't in love with her and that she just treated him as a kindly old man. He swore he was never jealous of any young man's attentions toward her. He continued to claim he didn't remember pursuing Dorothy or shooting her; all he could remember was that he had been suffering awful head pains.

Methever had nothing kind to say about his legal defense. He felt his lawyers, Davis & Morrison, had gone to trial too soon, before public indignation had sufficiently died down to insure a fair trial. His son, Ulysses, had scraped together the $1,000 to pay attorney fees. Methever didn't think he'd gotten his money's worth. The only good thing to come out of it was that Ulysses had decided to become an attorney. The younger Methever promised his father that, unlike his father's attorneys, he would make sure that justice was always pursued, right until the end.

On April 17, 1901, jailers reported that Methever refused to talk or even open his mouth to eat. He simply lay in his cell waiting to die. Was he really insane, or still trying to convince people he was? On May 10, 1901, Edward Methever was hanged at San Quentin prison, the first person from Long Beach to experience the death penalty.

Lew-is the Light and Murder

Long Beach's self proclaimed prophet, Lew-is the Light, was livid when he learned that murderer John W. Tinsley had requested in his suicide note that he, Lew-is the Light, serve as pall bearer at Tinsley's funeral. Lew-is knew Tinsley, but was outraged at the act Tinsley had committed. No amount of persuasion would convince Lew-is to lift a handle on the coffin of the wife murderer/suicide.

It had been an atrocious act. On December 27, 1900, John W. Tinsley met his estranged wife, Anna Pitman Tinsley, as she was leaving church. They argued and she tried to pull away. Angered, he grabbed her by the throat, hit her, threw her to the ground, put his knee to her breast and shot her through the head. He then committed suicide by shooting himself through the forehead.

Six days earlier Anna Tinsley had filed suit against her husband, claiming "the slick faker" abused her and had married her only for her money. She wanted him arrested for embezzlement and abuse. The couple had tied the knot on January 2, 1900, in Van Buren, Arkansas. The 35-year-old music teacher thought Tinsley wealthy; he had told her he was a Montana mining man worth $75,000. At the time Anna had $400 in cash and her house valued at $2,500. The couple decided to start a new life together in California. Settling in Los Angeles, Anna somehow ended up paying all the bills.

Tinsley told Anna his money was tied up and unavailable. In June the couple left for Mineral Springs, Texas, in hopes that Mrs. Tinsley's fragile health would improve. But in order to do so John needed money. He persuaded his wife to sell her Arkansas property for much less than what it was worth. He also got her to "prove her love" by buying him a $400 diamond ring and diamond stud. After trips to spas in Texas and Missouri, Tinsley told his wife the time was ripe, he could now recover his money. He would travel to Helena, Montana, where his $75,000 worth of property was located. Since it would take some time to wrap up his affairs, and since Anna's health was so poor, he told her it was best that he go alone. She believed his story and gave him $700 to make the trip.

But Tinsley never went to Montana. Instead, he wrote Anna saying she had been deceived and his $75,000 was all a myth. She returned to Los Angeles, almost penniless, but determined to go on. Anna tried to locate her husband through the police and other channels, but failed. She struggled along and with the help of a Methodist minister began teaching music once again. In late October 1900 she received a telegram from Tinsley asking if he could come back to her. Conscience or lack of money had gotten the best of him. Thinking she might recover some of her money, she agreed to see him. In the meantime she had learned he had been married in 1869 in Livingston County, Montana. Besides a wife he also had eight children and eleven grandchildren.

On November 3, 1900, the two met with her lawyer present. Tinsley told Anna he had disposed of the diamond ring and stud and that he only had $500 left, which was in a bank in Arkansas. They dickered and argued for quite awhile before her attorney got Tinsley to agree to pay her $325. The check bounced.

On December 25, 1900, when most were practicing "peace on earth, good will toward men," John Tinsley was plotting murder. He wrote a note saying he was going to take Anna's life on Christmas Day, and then take his own. If they couldn't live together they would at least die together. But Anna had a brief reprieve. He couldn't find her. And then at noon on December 27th, he traced her outside the Trinity M.E. Church in Los Angeles. Before witnesses he choked her, threw her to the sidewalk, pressed his knee on her breast and placed the muzzle of a big pistol against her right eye. He then pulled the trigger which sent a bullet straight through her brain. As the warm blood of his victim covered his body he turned his still smoking revolver upon himself, planted a bullet in his forehead, and fell dead beside the body of his supposed spouse. Like Alonzo Meyer before him, his suicide attempt was successful and he followed his wife to the grave.

When the coroner searched the murder's pockets he found a note which cleared up the mystery. On Christmas morning Tinsley had written:

"If I meet Mrs. Anna P. Tinsley today, I will take her life and then mine. If we can't live together then we will die together…Never let my body go inside of a Methodist church. I have little money: dig a hole, role a blanket around me like a Sioux Chief and plant me, for that is good enough for any Christian."

To this was added a postscript:

"Mrs. Tinsley has said a great deal publicly and through the press, in fact too much. I have nothing to say about our difficulties. The lord must be the judge who is right or who is wrong. In the Herald of the 22nd was an article that painted me very black, and hence the cause of this tragedy. That newspaper article, oh how unjust. Such articles are enough to unsettle a man's mind. I don't care to live now, but the perpetrator must go first, then I am willing to follow."

On December 27th he wrote on the same note:

"I expect to meet Mrs. T. at the M.E. church tomorrow and then I will do the work. I hope there is no one that will say I am crazy for my mind is as clear as it ever was. I am only a little forgetful. I am sound on religion. I have no fears of Hell or hopes of heaven. I hold no malice against anyone. I request that Britton Clark and Lee act as pall bearers, assisted by Lewey the Light. I would like to be buried by the side of Anna P. Tinsley, but I suppose my wishes will never be gratified. I am 58 years old the 12th of April next." (LA Times 12/28/1900).

Friends told reporters that Anna's health declined considerably once she married Tinsley. That was why he took her to the mineral springs in Texas and later to another curative spa in Missouri. Surprisingly, Anna's health improved once her husband left for his supposed mine in Montana. After thinking the matter over she came to the conclusion that Tinsley had attempted to get rid of her by slow poison, in order to get hold of all her money. She also learned that when he returned to Los Angeles without her he told acquaintances that she was dead, which he had probably expected since he poisoned her.

Later it was determined that Tinsley had divorced his first wife, Isabella, prior to his marriage to Anna. After accusing Isabella of having an affair with her doctor he threatened to kill them both. Isabella and the doctor escaped Tinsley's fury, but a Montana neighbor didn't. Following an intensive quarrel Tinsley killed the neighbor, but later received a pardon from Montana governor Potts.

Though Long Beach's "Lewey the Light," who Tinsley named as one of his pall bearers, declined the honor, stating he had no sympathy with suicide or murder, Lewey certainly had no problem with blackmail.

What do you do with a pest? That was the question Long Beach residents had to face when dealing with self proclaimed prophet "Lew-Is the Light." At first they received crank letters warning they must pay tithes to Lew-Is or bad luck would befall them. Whenever any news of personal tragedy was printed in the local newspapers Lew-Is wrote the unfortunate victim saying the misfortune would not have happened if the person had paid a tithe to Lew-Is. Lew-Is must have been successful in his campaign for tithes because he seemed to manage to live without work. No one in the city ever saw him perform any form of labor other than pestering the public with his annoying letters. Police Chief Williams was sure Lew-Is had made victims out of the superstitiously inclined who gave him money to get his "blessings."

When Tarrytown on Long Beach's amusement zone, the Pike, burned Lew-Is was on the street early the next morning peddling his little letters saying the fire was a judgment from the Lord because Lew-Is had not been paid his rightful tithes. Daily this self-styled Jesus sent newspapers mental wanderings boasting of his supernatural powers. But things got out of hand when Thomas Beck of 232 East Eighth Street had an epileptic seizure following receipt of a tithe demand from Lew-Is. Beck had received several letters from Lew-Is suggesting Beck pay him tithes in order to improve his health. Beck ignored the letters until he received the following:

"You seem to be a good natured man. I am going to twist your body out of shape and your mind with it, so that you shall not be able to think right or be any wiser than the heathen idolaters around you. Thus I shall be able to drag you down to death. If you pay up you will understand and the evil spirit will depart. Ignorance of the law is no excuse. It is as easy to pay the tithe to Lew-Is The Lord of the life of your body and soul, as it is to pay the gardener. Faithfully and financially yours. LEW-IS." (*Long Beach Press* 1/2/1908)

This missive was enough to give Beck a seizure and have the police step in. Chief of Police Williams said that unless Lew-Is the Light made a solemn vow to stop his letter writing campaigns he would try to have him declared legally insane. If the sanity commission didn't put him away, the chief said he would keep him locked up permanently on a charge of being a public nuisance. On January 29, 1908, Lew-Is the Light saw the light. After a severe talking to by local police he agreed to stop his letter writing and claiming he was Jesus. But Lew-Is had a hard time keeping his pledge.

On June 3, 1908, Chief Williams, true to his word, had Lew-Is taken before Judge Brayton. Lew-Is had been scaring people again including young Dick Harover who had fallen from a church steeple. Lew-Is told the boy that had he been paying tithes to Lew-Is the injury would never have happened.

When questioned by the judge Lew-Is declared he was "God Almighty the Eternal Ruler" and that the court had no right to pass judgment upon him. Judge Brayton sentenced Lew-Is to thirty days in the county jail for vagrancy and told him to leave the area when he was released. On the way to his new residence, Lew-Is entertained policeman with stories about how the Bixby Hotel disaster would never have happened (story reported in chapter *Murderous Architecture*), nor would the chicken ranch on Signal Hill have gone up in flames, had people listened to him. In his new abode Lew-Is the Light was now in darkness. Upon release he headed to Massachusetts and when the weather turned cold he returned to Los Angeles. Along the way he continued to annoy people with his parables.

A Fiery Death

The Goodnight's final resting place up on Signal Hill provided a stunning view of not only the ocean but the Palos Verdes peninsula. On a clear day Catalina Island was visible twenty-five miles away. Lenora had preceded her husband to this picturesque site and he had followed a few months later. One of their illustrious neighbors was William Willmore, the founder of Long Beach. They all shared the same address: Long Beach Municipal Cemetery. Lenora had died returning to a burning building to retrieve her paltry savings. Her husband died from burns incurred trying to save her.

Mrs. Goodnight's tragic end came in the early morning of July 6, 1903. The couple and their son were living in a building at First and Canal streets in Wilmington when a fire of incendiary origin broke out. Mrs. Goodnight was burned to death, her husband Tom was badly scorched on the face and body; their son Ed had his face and hands badly singed by the intense heat. Jack Slater and H.J. Miller, who made desperate attempts to rescue Mrs. Goodnight, also suffered extensive burns. The only one to escape uninjured was Alexander Axelrod, who had a dry good store in the building. He had watched the fire with folded arms, making no attempt whatsoever to help save Mrs. Goodnight.

The building was an old structure containing three stores in the front and numerous rooms in the back. Tom Goodnight had a milkshake and fruit stand on the south side of the building; next to him was Alexander Axelrod, with his dry goods store. The room on the north side was unoccupied; the last tenant had been a baker.

On that Sunday morning around 2 a.m. Henry Torst, a barber, was returning home from a dance. He saw flames issuing from the old structure in which the Goodnights and Axelrod both lived and worked. Torst fired his gun, awakening the town. Some folks, still in their bed clothes, sped to the scene. Soon 70-year-old Thomas B. Goodnight rushed from the building in his night clothes. Right behind him was his 65-year-old wife. Witnesses said Lenora suddenly stopped. Without a word to anyone she rushed into the burning building. It seemed she had remembered the hoard of money she had hidden. Goodnight, realizing what his wife had done, dashed toward the door to stop her, but he was repelled by a wall of fire. As he backed away from the inferno he accidentally closed the door, locking it from the inside. Mrs. Goodnight could be heard trying to get out through the door, but she could not turn the fiery red lock.

Tom Goodnight and neighbor H.J. Miller frantically continued trying to break the door down from the outside, but to no avail. As Mrs. Goodnight tried desperately to escape the flame filled room, Miller crashed through the window. A grisly sight awaited him. He saw Mrs. Goodnight, a pillar of flame, totter and fall. Miller was forced to retreat before the heat, but he was soon replaced by Jack Slater who tried to drag the burning woman from the building through the broken window.

During all of this Alex Axelrod did nothing. When it was over, and nothing remained of the building, the crowd went after Axelrod eager to hang him. They were sure he had deliberately set the fire to collect insurance money. His stunned silence and refusal to run calmed the lynch mob. They would let the courts decide his fate.

When asked to describe what happened, a badly burned Goodnight said he awoke to the glare of the fire in his room and immediately felt the heat. He roused his wife and together they went out through the front door. He was positive the fire came from the direction of Axelrod's rooms.

When the fire was extinguished and the ashes examined, investigators found a melted dollar, three halves, and several nickels. All that remained of the $155 Mrs. Goodnight had given her life to save.

Alex Axelrod was exonerated. It was shown he had no insurance, and he had no dislike for any of the Goodnight family. However, the discovery of a jug of oil led the jury to decide that someone had purposely committed the devilish deed. Who it was remains a mystery to this day.

Mystery still surrounds the Goodnight's final resting place. One mystery is how old the Municipal Cemetery at the northwest corner of Orange and Willow really is. The oldest marked grave is that of a Milton F. Neece who was buried there in 1878 at the age of 17. But old timers back in the 1950's remembered a man who used to visit the cemetery in the 1930's. The man told the sexton his father had been buried there years earlier when the man was just a boy. Since the man appeared to be in his 80's, it could push the date of the cemetery as far back as the 1850's.

Even the old record books aren't of any help; they were kept so poorly that there is even doubt about who is buried in the graves. When the city took over the cemetery in 1903 from the Long Beach Cemetery Association, they found the record books were a mess. The early caretakers thought all they were responsible for was appointing a sexton to look after the property, but several of the sextons could not read or write and their attempt at bookkeeping and posting records was amusing at best. Many lots had been sold, but there was no record of the owners. When the Department of the City Clerk took over the record keeping in 1906 they discovered one instance where five bodies had been buried in one grave and several lots sold three or four times.

In his spare time Deputy City Clerk Paine would get out the old map of the cemetery and devote a few hours trying to untangle the bookkeeping nightmare. At one time, according to the records, one man was buried in eight different lots. Paine swore he would not rest until he finally allotted each corpse to its proper grave.

Hopefully Paine is at rest. His work of sorting out cemetery records has been taken on by Mark Christoffels of the Public Works Department and dedicated volunteer Marie Sorenson. A cemetery tour is held each October by the Historical Society of Long Beach.

Music and Murder

Today, and at the turn of the 20th century, people come to Long Beach to have good wholesome fun. Visitors in 1903 had much to entertain them. There was the huge whale on display in Pacific Park, the entertainment zone known as the Pike, theaters, a pier, a pavilion, a beautiful beach and, most importantly, plenty of music. Bands such as the Long Beach Marine Band, the American Band and the Italian Band played a tremendous role in attracting people to Long Beach. Many musicians were employed by private concerns like the Majestic Skating Rink, working for a percentage of the receipts or on a subscription basis. One of these musicians was Olin Castle.

Olin and his widowed mother arrived in Long Beach in January 1903. Twenty-six-year-old Olin had found work playing the bass viol in two Long Beach bands. His 22-year-old fiancée, Lillian de Talent, followed in mid April. The couple soon married.

Lillian and Olin asked the Reverend Adkinson of the Methodist Episcopal Church for a simple wedding ceremony; no flowers, no attendants, and no publicity. It was hoped that these precautions would keep the press at bay. It wasn't that the couple was hiding their marriage, they simply knew that the name of Olin Castle would conjure up the image of a dreadful crime, one in which his first wife had been murdered less than a week after their marriage. Olin's name had been in every newspaper of nearly every city town and village in the United States for the last few years. Now he was marrying Lillian, a journalist who had written about his first wife's shocking murder at Eldorado, Kansas, in June 1900.

Olin's nightmare began the morning of June 22, 1900, when neighbors of the newlyweds heard sounds of a scuffle, followed by screams. Rushing to the Castle house they found Clara Castle lying on the floor, her throat slashed and her arms and breasts cut by the razor Jessie Morrison held in her hand. Jessie Morrison also appeared slightly cut. What had happened?

Only the two women had been in the room. It looked like they had fought, but who had initiated the attack? Clara could not speak because of the gaping wound in her throat. But before she died she nodded in agreement when asked if Jessie Morrison had attacked her savagely with the razor. A statement was written to that effect and Clara signed it before her final breath.

Jessie Morrison, however, had a different story, one she stuck to through three trials. Jessie claimed she had been passing along the street in front of the Castle home when Clara called her in and assaulted her with the deadly razor. In fear for her life, Jessie somehow found the strength to wrestle the razor from Clara Castle's hands. Mrs. Castle's wounds, Jessie claimed, were administered in self defense.

This was the beginning of the case which would become one of the most widely noted in the criminal annals of the United States up to that time. Readers throughout the nation eagerly read how both women loved the same handsome musician. It was a story out of a romance novel.

Jessie Morrison and Clara Wiley, who would become Olin Castle's bride, both worked in the same music store in which Olin was a clerk. Jessie stated throughout her trials that Olin had been very attentive to her, even though she was ten years his senior, and that he had jilted her in favor of Clara. But Olin still loved her Jessie testified, her hand on a Bible. He continued to send her love letters and presents after he became engaged. When Jessie told Clara this, Clara became upset. So upset, Jessie went on, that Clara vowed she would murder Jessie.

Olin told another story. He said he had just been nice to Jessie, after all they worked together. Somehow Jessie got the wrong idea. She had pursued him, he had tried to evade her, but she wouldn't give up. None of what she said about his continued gifts and attention was true. She was delusional and insanely jealous of Clara, whom he loved. Jessie had vowed to make their life together miserable and she had succeeded.

When Jessie broke down in tears at her first trial and the judge, obviously moved by Jessie's sobs and perhaps because Jessie's father, also a judge, was a good friend, said Clara's dying declaration was simply a concoction of men trying to convict an innocent girl. He declared all the evidence in the case circumstantial and Mrs. Castle's dying statement suspect. Because of this blatant favoritism, the trial resulted in a hung jury. A second judge and jury found Jessie guilty and sentenced her to 5 years in prison. But Jessie and her lawyer father wanted complete acquittal. They appealed the decision. In 1902 her third trial began. She should have served her five years; the third trial also found her guilty but upped her sentence to 25 years imprisonment. Exhausting further appeals, Jessie began her 25-year sentence on June 10, 1903; a wonderful wedding present for Olin and his new bride.

What is it with musicians, most men want to know, that makes women go wild? Jessie Morrison had killed for Olin Castle. But Olin wasn't the only Long Beach musician that drove women into a frenzy. Nicola Donatelli, the leader of Long Beach's Italian Band, was certainly a heart throb. Women flocked to his concerts. Twenty-nine-year-old

Donatelli, a native of Naples, Italy, played nearly every instrument in his band in a "masterful" way. But it wasn't just this talent that had women drooling. His charm, good looks, suave demeanor and Italian accent added to his allure.

Though successful with women, Donatelli had less success with his band. In January 1906 Donatelli's musicians demanded his resignation as director, labeling him abusive and tyrannical; they compared him to the Russian czar. Faced with finding all new band members or just one new director, band manager Domenico Gattone fired Donatelli. Gattone was sure he could find a new leader, equally renowned for Long Beach.

Twenty-six-year-old Marco Vessella was lured to Long Beach to head the newly named Royal Italian Band. Educated in Rome under the tutelage of his famous uncle, Alasandro Vessella, the director of the 100 piece Band of Rome, young Marco was highly respected among the Italian musicians he directed. However, Vessella lacked one thing. He did not have Donatelli's sex appeal. Donatelli's female admirers were not happy with his removal from the Italian Band. Though they said they preferred Donatelli's musical talents over Vessella's, the truth was they missed his romantic good looks and charm. Marco Vessella was O.K., but he was no Donatelli.

Attendance at the band concerts dwindled. Long Beach city fathers believed if they got Donatelli to return he would attract enough female fans to make the concerts profitable. In August 1906 they decided to bring Donatelli back from Venice for a special Long Beach performance. However, when word of Donatelli's coming reached the Royal Italian Band they rebelled. For the sake of peace, Donatelli's contract to appear again in Long Beach was revoked.

Diminished audiences meant diminished revenue. Long Beach needed a band to attract visitors who would support local businesses and boost the city's economy. But how to pay these musicians remained a point of debate for several years. The issue was finally settled when, on August 30, 1909, an ordinance was passed making the musicians Long Beach city employees. With this stroke of a pen Long Beach became the first city in the nation with its own truly "municipal" band.

With Donatelli's departure the female set in Long Beach soon found another romantic musician to swoon over. Bud Belden, the snare drummer of the band playing at the Majestic Skating Rink, had a thing for young girls. Belden took advantage of his handsome good looks, alluring smile and sex appeal. After his concerts he was frequently seen with a very young miss strolling through the Pike arm in arm, disappearing for a time behind a dark building. This did not go over well with parents. On August 13, 1906, Belden was shot at by the mother of a 13-year-old-girl he allegedly raped. He escaped the irate mother, but not the stepfather.

That hot August evening the parents of the young girl lay in wait for the married Belden to come out of the Majestic Skating Rink. When he did, Mrs. Wilson angrily pulled out a gun and fired two shots at the musician. She had been waiting on a customer at the family's confectionery booth on the Pike when she glanced up and saw Belden across the way. With a muttered oath she reached beneath the counter, seized a revolver and dashed toward Belden, firing two shots at him. Neither hurt him. Belden fled with Mr. Wilson, carrying a double barreled shot gun, in hot pursuit. Bystanders prevented a shooting, but Wilson, angered by the assault upon his stepdaughter, said he would finish the job later. Later law enforcement officers arrested Belden, charging him with the rape. In turn, the drummer filed a counter claim against Mr. & Mrs. Wilson claiming they tried to kill him.

On August 29, 1906, twenty-six-year-old Belden, released on bail, was on his way to court for the preliminary hearing on the charge of committing an aggravated criminal assault on Nathalie Wilson. While Belden was walking south on Pine Nathalie's stepfather confronted him. William Wilson drew his long barreled revolver and fired one shot at close range into Belden.

According to witnesses, Belden gave a cry of pain and terror, ran a few steps, circled around a post and fell in the gutter at William Wilson's feet. Wilson stepped forward, and holding the revolver steady with both hands, pumped three more shots into the dying man. Though the last three shots were not fatal, they further mutilated Belden's body and caused the man to moan and convulse. One bullet entered the top of Belden's left shoulder, shattering it and coming out underneath; the second made only a flesh wound in the right arm, while the last shot entered the right arm above the elbow and ended up lodged in the shoulder blade. Witnesses stood spellbound and stunned until the fourth shot was fired. Finally contractor Richard Loynes seized the murderer and swung him around. Only then did the fury leave Wilson and he stood in stunned silence.

Belden was hastily carried across the street into Jackson's drug store where Doctors Lawton, Hamman and Bowman futilely tried to save his life. He died within 15 minutes. On being taken to police headquarters Wilson shouted "My God! I've stood it as long as I could." (*Evening Tribune* 8/29/1906). Six extra shells were found in Wilson's pocket. The community was stunned. Long Beach had established a reputation for peace and quiet and nothing like this had occurred since Dorothy McKee's murder in 1900.

Later, Wilson told why he shot to kill:

"It was about seven weeks ago that Belden met Nathalie first and noticed her," Wilson said. "I did not notice anything serious until about a week before the child confessed, and then my suspicions amounted to almost nothing, for she is only a child. Then I noticed that he was in the habit of talking with her near our stand on the strand, when she was left in charge while her mother and I went home for our meals. I called the child aside and told her that she was still a little girl and too young to have a sweetheart. 'When you are grown up and old enough, it will be my business to see that you have a sweetheart that is worth while,' I said to her. I warned her to keep away from Belden, but my suspicions grew apace. I found that he had laid out a deliberate course to capture the affections of the child, and that he had been successful. He had sent her presents, and beginning by pretense of friendship, he had wormed his way into her graces until she allowed him to put his arm around her and kiss her. From that it went, as I found out too late, to worse things. Two or three nights later I kept watch. I saw him walk with her, his arm clasped around her, from their meeting place to the corner of the building where we roomed. He had been there before: making love to her. I questioned the girl. She told me how he had gradually made her care for him, and then she confessed to everything. She admitted that the man had taken advantage of her innocence, not once, but twice."
(LA Times 8/31/1906)

Wilson went to trial for the murder of Belden and was found not guilty by a jury of his peers. The moment after the verdict was rendered the quiet of the courtroom was broken by applause and cries of approval. Conservative Long Beach folk thought Wilson a hero.

Murderous Architecture

Ever since Long Beach's luxurious Long Beach Hotel had been destroyed by fire in 1888 the city had been desperate for a new high class hotel. Thirteen years later, with the arrival of millionaire Charles Drake, it looked like a first rate hotel was again going to be a possibility.

If Rancho Los Cerritos' Jotham Bixby was known as the "father" of Long Beach, and William E. Willmore as the "founder," Col. Charles Rivers Drake must be remembered as the "promoter" of Long Beach. Virtually ignored in the early written histories of the city because of his opposition to the harbor, Drake deserves a special place in Long Beach's history. At the age of fifty-seven Drake decided to retire and move to Southern California, but as a descendent of Sir Francis Drake, the explorer blood in his veins would not let him rest. He was one of the first men to envision the growth of Long Beach and the amusement potential of the beach frontage.

With powerful backers such as the Bixbys, Flints and Clarks behind him, Drake formed the Long Beach Hotel Company in 1904 to build a luxury hotel. The $500,000 structure located at the foot of Magnolia Avenue, on property purchased from Drake, would have a stunning view of the ocean. It was to be five stories tall topped with a roof garden, stage, orchestra, alcoves and tropical plants. The first floor would contain offices, a dining room, grand reception hall, and billiard parlor. The floors above would be guest rooms and suites, each with its own private bath. The hotel was situated near Long Beach's Pine Avenue Pier and adjacent to Drake's bustling, active, Coney Island style midway called the Pike. Here there was a playground and day nursery for children, a carrousel, roller skating rink, a scenic railway (roller coaster), and a monster Ferris wheel, 50 feet high, the largest ever seen in this part of the country.

What would this new luxury hotel that Long Beach had so long waited for be called? A contest was held and Frank Wyncoop provided the winning name—the Hotel Bixby. But the name would be discretely changed to the Hotel Virginia after a devastating tragedy.

On November 9, 1906, people miles away heard what sounded like the roaring of the sea as an avalanche of twisted iron and cement went crashing through the fifth and sixth floors of the center wing of the new hotel. A woman, who was walking on the sidewalk opposite the half-built structure, thought it was a tidal wave and ran for her life to get away from the ocean front.

The collapse began with a slight downward heave. Some workmen on the top floor felt the movement and fled into the wings and were saved. Then pulverized cement began to stream downward until the whole center of the building went roaring down in a cloud of dust that rose high over the structure like smoke from a big fire. One hundred and forty artisans and laborers were working in various parts of the structure when, without warning, the sixth and fifth floors tore loose from the west wing. Ten workmen died and ten more were seriously injured.

There was one hero, an African American later identified as D.I. Hoyt, who, while the building was still trembling, climbed into the smoking debris and calmly issued orders to clear the scene. Shortly thereafter help arrived. The Long Beach militia and police kept the crowd back while soldiers looked for the dead and wounded. The Salt Lake railway whirled in a special train with a huge steam crane from the water front, while the Pacific Electric rushed in Mexican and Japanese workers to help search for survivors.

Everyone did what they could to help. One woman hurried home to strip sheets from her beds to wrap the dead victims of the tragedy. Two other women stood throughout the night waiting to draw the sheets over the dead faces as the bodies were dragged out from the ruins. Other women stood hour after hour at long tables handling out coffee and sandwiches to the workers.

It was agonizing to hear cries coming from under the debris, cries that grew fainter and fainter and then stopped all together before help could get to them. The steam crane loaned from the harbor lifted one corpse—a headless trunk. Some victims could not even be recognized as human.

One woman came begging for word of her husband. When police asked her name she stared in bewilderment, and then sank sobbing to the ground. She was so distraught she had forgotten her own name. One of the most ghastly sights, the *Times* reported, was the timekeeper standing on a pile of debris, checking the names of the dead as they were carried out of the ruins. It was like the roll call of death. The names on the list included: Carpenters Luis Felker, B.A. Burrell, Louis Philips, Carlton Brashear, F. Norton, Afton Bejanson, Albert Harley; Richard Perkins, stripper; Roscoe Collins, tile layer; Alvin Deshazer, laborer. There was one seeming miracle. Young Ed Nicholson fell six stories and survived unharmed.

Architect Austin said there was no question that the collapse was caused solely by removing the fifth floor supports too soon. Supports were supposed to remain in place for 30 days, but foremen later admitted they had removed them on the eighteenth day. This, the coroner's jury ruled, was the cause of the collapse. There was no criminal liability. The collapse was due to taking away supports before the concrete was properly set.

Work resumed a short time later and, in 1907, the name of the hotel was quietly changed from the Hotel Bixby to the Hotel Virginia. Opening in 1908 the Virginia would be the Grand Dame of Long Beach hotels for many years to come. Sadly, it would be torn down a few days before the devastating March 10, 1933, Long Beach earthquake. Many later wondered if the earthquake was punishment for the sin of destroying such a lovely structure.

The Irish had their holiday, Saint Patrick's Day, the Italians Columbus Day, why not a holiday for the British? Since 1838, when Queen Victoria ascended the thrown, May 24th had been celebrated as the queen's birthday. After her death in 1901 her subjects still wanted to continue the celebration, but they changed the name to Empire Day to commemorate the expansion of the British Empire during their beloved queen's reign. On May 24, 1913, the first Empire Day in Southern California was celebrated. Twenty-five thousand British and former British subjects gathered in Long Beach for a festive day which turned into one of the worst tragedies in Southern California history.

The *Daily Telegram* of May 23, 1913, described what was supposed to have happened:

"The greatest British celebration ever held on foreign soil. That is what the committee in charge of the arrangements for the big Empire Day celebration to be held in this city tomorrow expects the fete to be. From all over the Southland will come those who formerly lived under the British flag. Drawing card features of the day will be the presence of the British man-of-war, Shearwater, 60 of whose sailors will act as an escort for the

veterans in the parade; there will be a big program of athletic stunts, national games, the parade, music and the natural attractions of Long Beach. The parade will be elaborate, with several floats each representing dominions or possessions of the English nation, the participants of each float being natives of the that particular country represented. The parade will reach the auditorium where speeches will be made. Five hundred dollars worth of prizes will be given to the winners of the various contests."

What was to have been a day of joy turned into one of tragedy when a rotten girder outside the entrance of the municipal auditorium gave way.

It was just at the close of the parade when disaster struck. The marchers, and those in vehicles, turned from Ocean Avenue to the top level of the two-tiered Pine Avenue Pier on their way to the auditorium for a celebration program. The main entrance to the auditorium became blocked by the crowd, and those in the rear pressed forward in such large numbers that they caused a rotten 4 x 14 girder to break. Masses of people fell through or on top of another crowd which packed the lower deck; then the floor of the lower deck also gave way, tumbling people to the sand and water below. Thirty-eight people died and approximately 200 were injured.

The *Long Beach Press* reported:

"What must go down in history as the most terrible disaster in the annals of Southern California, made gruesome history at 11:33 o'clock this morning when a four foot square section of the Municipal auditorium fell to the sand below. Heart rending scenes, never before equaled in the history of Long Beach were enacted on the beach as the dead and living were carried out and tenderly laid on the sand. Many begged piteously to die. A lad of ten years was seen to pass away in his mother's arms, as she

was raising a glass of brandy to his lips. A broken-hearted father carried the limp and almost lifeless form of his fourteen-month-old baby to the steps to hunt for a doctor. His wife lay on the beach with her life crushed out."
(LB Press 5/24/1913)

In 1943 Signal Hill fireman Fred Paine recalled the tragedy for the *Press Telegram* on the thirtieth anniversary of the disaster:

"I stood at the corner of Ocean and Pine and watched the parade go by, then followed the crowd down Pine to the auditorium, where a program was to be given. About 500 persons were waiting for the doors to open, jammed on the section of the double-decked pier that led to the auditorium, when it collapsed. I lay for an hour and a half pinned in the wreckage, while police, firemen and rescuers worked to free us. A dead man, heavyset, lay on top of me all that time. His neck must have been broken. I saw a woman badly hurt. She was still living. Some victims were praying to live, some praying to die." (Press-Telegram 5/23/1943)

It took a full ten minutes for the crowds on the pier, only a few hundred feet away from the disaster, to realize what had happened. When the fire chief's auto came dashing up to assist in the relief work, many thought the fire department was giving an exhibition as part of the festivities.

Long Beach felt responsible for the tragedy. Doctors donated their services free of charge. $10,000 was quickly raised to aid the victims. The following statement was issued in the *Daily Telegram* on May 26, 1913:

"The citizens of Long Beach will courageously and promptly meet every responsibility and humane demand growing out of Saturday's awful tragedy.

The dead will be given proper burial and the wounds of the injured will be cared for by the best obtainable medical and nursing skill. The needs of every surviving victim will be promptly and heartily supplied. There will be no red tape to handicap our people in demonstrating to the world, that we entertain a full understanding of our obligations to suffering humanity and propose to meet them with decision and sympathetic candor."

The Citizens' Relief Committee was true to their word. Arthur Lett, a former conductor on the Pacific Electric who lost his wife and two of his three children, was one example. His slender savings could not cover funeral expenses nor buy lots in the cemetery. The Committee provided money to cover the burials and purchase cemetery plots.

Twelve-year-old Margaret Reed was the 37th victim of the pier disaster. On June 6, 1913, Margaret was buried at Long Beach's Sunnyside Cemetery. Among the mourners was a slight, simply dressed man who mingled with the group. No one suspected he was a postal inspector from Los Angeles there to arrest Isaac Reed, Margaret's father, should Isaac come out of hiding to attend the funeral. Isaac Reed was accused of taking $1,072 in money order funds when he was postmaster at Dale, in San Bernardino County. Gambling was the cause of the crime. Just before he sent his wife and daughter to Long Beach and then disappeared, Isaac told them he would be gone for a long time. He confessed that he was harassed by debt and did not intend to come back until he made enough money to repay what he had stolen. But Isaac did not appear at his daughter's funeral. Neither did Margaret's mother, hospitalized with a dislocated shoulder suffered in the Empire Day tragedy.

A three man board of inquiry was immediately set up with local architect W. Horace Austin selected to represent Long Beach. Their findings were presented to a grand jury. On June 2nd the grand jury announced the following decision:

"Every one knows the accident was caused by a rotten girder and every one knows the girder was not properly inspected. I will let this matter simmer a while. If Long Beach had taken 100 years to grow as much as it has in ten weeks, the accident probably would not have happened, but when cities grow fast people have a tendency to keep on doing things in a village way." (Daily Telegram 6/2/1913)

Long Beach was the fastest growing city in the nation from 1900 to 1910. Its population had increased almost 800%, growing from 2,252 people in 1900 to 17,809 in 1910. The finding of the grand jury was that the city had grown too fast to keep up with all of its civic responsibilities. And it was continuing to grow. In 1913 the population was 29,000. In 1914 it had skyrocketed to 46,000, a 60% increase in one year alone.

Attorneys advised the city that they were not financially responsible for the disaster, but Long Beach citizens believed they had a moral responsibility for the tragedy. On June 18th, Long Beach residents overwhelmingly voted to add a special tax levy of .20 cents to each $100 of their assessed property valuation. This was to take care of the sick, helpless and dependent victims of the disaster. In July, with the money raised by this special tax, the city paid out $24,181.68 on claims presented from the auditorium disaster. But more claims were to come, and even this special tax would not cover them all.

Many did not agree with the grand jury decision absolving Long Beach of the financial obligation towards the victims. A Superior Court decision ruled that victims, or their survivors, had a one year statute of limitations in which to file claims against the city. By May

23, 1914, nearly 200 suits totaling more than $3,000,000 were brought to Superior Court. The Chafor case, filed by George E. Chafor over the death of his wife Edith, was the first claim brought to the court. It was to set a precedent for all the rest.

On July 9, 1914, after 18 days of testimony and five hours of deliberation the jury awarded $7,500 in damages for the death of Mrs. Chafor. The city immediately appealed the case to the California Supreme Court listing five reasons the verdict should be overturned: that the city was engaged in a governmental enterprise; that the auditorium was constructed in a public street and by express act of the city charter Long Beach was exempted from liability; that the structure was partly constructed on the tidelands of the state, which the state held in trust for the public, and therefore it could not be the property of the city; that the use of the auditorium was gratuitously loaned to the committee holding the entertainment and that the city was not responsible for the condition of the building; that the evidence conclusively showed that the city never consented to the holding of the large assemblage but that consent was given by the City Council, the Board of Public Works only having the authority, and that the board never gave its consent. All other claims from the disaster were put on hold until the Supreme Court verdict.

In May 1916 the Supreme Court ruled Long Beach was not liable in the Empire Day Auditorium disaster. The issue surrounded the question as to whether the city, in constructing and building the pier and auditorium, exercised a governmental or political power, or a proprietary or corporate one. They decreed Long Beach exercised a governmental power and therefore was not liable. In February 1917 the California Supreme Court reversed their decision. They realized their prior ruling exempted municipalities from liability, thus putting them beyond the reach of the law.

By mid April 1918 the city had settled all 174 damage suits of the disaster. The total amount of money sought in these claims totaled $3,447,005.08. The City Attorney managed to settle all cases for $372,162.70. The problem was that the city did not have any money. On February 26, 1919, the State Supreme Court affirmed the right of the City of Long Beach to issue bonds to pay the auditorium damage judgments. Now the claims could be settled.

Some good did come out of the disaster—romance. On January 1, 1915, Clement C. Bush, 76 years old, who lost his wife in the disaster, married Mrs. Kate Ustes, aged 48, who was his nurse.

It had started out in humble circumstances, a pretty green bungalow on Jessie Street that served a dual purpose. On Sundays a wooden box was brought in and used as a pulpit, and boards placed on boxes to provide seats for the 8-12 youngsters who came for religious instruction. But it soon became too small to accommodate all of Long Beach's burgeoning population.

In 1904 Max Bridges, a staunch Methodist, moved into the area. He had just built a 28 x 400 foot structure at California and Tenth Street and offered it free of charge to the Sunday school. Now Central Long Beach children, who used to spend their Sundays playing ball on vacant lots, would have a permanent place to go to learn Christian values. But adults, too, needed a place of worship. Within months a full fledged Methodist church was established and the property purchased from Mr. Bridges at a very reasonable cost. The Sunday school building was remodeled and enlarged. But was this building, now a church, a portal for death?

Could a church be responsible for helping kill? That's the question many members of the Central Methodist Episcopal church asked the morning of August 18, 1915. Four people had just lost their lives and two others were injured. The jitney bus they were traveling in had crashed into a Salt Lake passenger train at the corner of East Tenth and California streets, right in front of the church. Had the building somehow been responsible? Had it hidden the approaching train from the bus? Was it another case of murderous architecture? It would be up to a jury to decide.

The bus had skidded into the train killing jitney passengers Alonzo Billings, Mrs. M.J. Mulvihill, Rebecca Weilenman and her 13-year-old daughter Gladys. Though the speed limit of jitneys was twenty miles per hour, Hendrick Mundy, the jitney driver said he was driving fast because he was afraid he would lose his job. The driver who was quickest got the fare, and Mundy had a quota to make if he was to keep his job driving for W.E. Pickering, who ran a line of jitney buses in Long Beach.

The jitney scheme of using automobiles to transport passengers had arrived in Long Beach in March 1914 with A.H. Kirkendall from Phoenix, Arizona. The idea had originated three years earlier to handle traffic in the Arizona capital, which didn't have a massive street car system like Los Angeles. Here the pay-to-ride motor car was a boon to the residents of the newly opened housing tracts out from Phoenix. Long Beach, however, had the highly efficient Pacific Electric rail line, but Kirkendall decided to give the Arizona idea a go. He began his Long Beach operation using his Ford to carry people from Ocean and Pine along East Fourth Street. Within two weeks other auto owners quickly adopted the idea of using their own vehicles to make money.

The term "jitney" is credited to Long Beach's John H. Meteer who coined the name from the one-time colloquial term for a 5-cent piece. Since the cost of carrying passengers in these auto buses was 5-cents, the term stuck. By July 1914 the jitney business had spread throughout Southern California, by December there were more than 1,000 cars-for-hire operating in Los Angeles alone. Plastering their autos with signs, the jitney drivers followed the courses of different street car lines picking up passengers along the way and running ahead of the electric cars. The drivers often traveled along the crowded streets, close to the curb and stopped between the sidewalk and a street car, almost forcing passengers to get into their autos.

Anna McPherson who with driver Hendrick Mundy escaped serious injury that August 1915 day, told authorities Mundy waved to a woman and little girl at 4th and Pine. He said they were his wife and child, and that he had to quickly get back to them. As he turned into Tenth Street from Pine he sped up. Mrs. McPherson said the ride was the fastest she had ever taken. As she was about to ask him to slow down she felt the collision. She didn't remember hearing any bells or whistles coming from the train. All she could recall was almost going under the wheels of the train and then being thrown out. When she regained consciousness she was lying beside Mrs. Weilenman, who was dying in a huge pool of blood. Conductor J.E. Edwards of the Salt Lake train said the jitney bus seemed to rush right into the engine, though the train engineer blew the whistle as usual as he approached the Tenth Street crossing.

It was up to a jury to decide if the church site or Mr. Mundy was responsible for the tragedy. On August 18, 1915, the jury took a trip to the scene of the accident to find out whether the Central Methodist Church building prevented automobile drivers from seeing an approaching train. After viewing the situation from many angles, they decided that had Mr. Mundy been driving at moderate speed he could have seen the train in time to stop his car. The church was exonerated.

Following these deaths the Long Beach Public Safety Commission passed an ordinance compelling all jitney bus drivers to come to a full stop before they crossed a railroad track. A "wig-wag" signal was also erected at the dangerous Tenth and California grade crossing.

Murder of a Policeman

Although Long Beach had some sort of police protection ever since the city was incorporated in 1888, the first "real" department operating under a regular Chief of Police, with patrolmen walking beats and giving the city 24-hour protection, was not established until 1908. This graduation of the city out of the "city marshal" class was considered an epoch in the growth and progress of Long Beach.

Elected to office January 17, 1908, Thomas W. Williams, in effect, became Long Beach's first "real" Chief of Police operating under powers given him by the new city charter. Williams was familiar with the job, having served as marshal several times.   Before, city marshals were assisted by one regular paid deputy and as many special deputies as they cared to buy badges for. There was no jail in the early days and when a criminal was captured he was usually locked in the strongest shed in town until he could be transported to the county jail. It was not until 1899 that a small iron cell was installed in the rear of city hall. The jailer also acted as custodian of two hand drawn fire carts.

The first attempt to establish a police headquarters was made by City Marshal George Young in 1906 when he hired Fred Kutz to act as desk sergeant and keep the department records. Until then Young had desk space in a real estate office. Other officers were added to the marshal's force during Young's administration. Another major accomplishment of Young's stay in office was getting Long Beach a new steel jail. It had two corridors and seven cells, each six by seven feet in size and seven feet in height and, most importantly, it was guaranteed to be impregnable to saws. This modern prison also had a separate cell for women, and one was padded for any prisoner suspected of insanity.

In 1908 Williams appointed Jotham Bixby's daughter Fanny as police matron, a post she held for several years. She was the first police matron in the United States and served without pay. Her specialty was "reclaiming boys and girls from waywardness." Williams also established the detective bureau and installed the first police call boxes in the city. His officers worked 12 hour shifts and called into headquarters every 30 minutes. Until Williams became head of the department investigation had been a hit or miss proposition, the entire department participating in investigations.

Williams resigned as Chief of Police in 1910 and was replaced by Clarence Moyer. It was during Moyer's term as police chief that the Police Department suffered its first fatality. On Sunday, March 17, 1912, 60-year-old officer Thomas C. Borden became the first Long Beach policeman to be killed in the line of duty.

Returning from church that Saint Patrick's Day evening, Matilda Borden stopped to talk to a neighbor as Tom continued to their home at 226 E. 10th Street. He quickly saw that something was amiss. Their front door was open and someone was coming out. Matilda heard her husband calmly ask someone what he was doing; many later wondered if Borden's calm demeanor indicated the killer was someone he knew. Startled, the burglar turned a gun on Borden, shooting Borden with Borden's own revolver. The police officer had left his loaded gun lying in the open when he left the house with his wife to attend church.

Matilda Borden's screams brought swift action. Neighbors, attracted by the gunfire and cries, came and carried the wounded officer into a nearby house and called an ambulance. Tom Borden was rushed to the Long Beach Sanitarium where he died just as the ambulance reached the entrance. An autopsy later revealed that two bullets had entered Tom Borden's body. The first hit Borden in the stomach just above the navel. This wound caused the police officer to bend in pain. The second shot, which entered the top of the head, traveled downward, splitting in two; one half emerging under the jaw and the other penetrating the chest and lodging in the lung.

Within minutes of the shooting the police were in hot pursuit. They retrieved Borden's pistol holster in a vacant lot near 11th and Locust and later they found his handcuffs. They also discovered a safety razor and a bunch of pass keys in the woods. Evidently the murderer didn't want to be caught with any evidence. From the place where the holster was found footprints led to American Avenue where the killer turned north, running over lawns, but keeping close to homes to provide cover. Finally the murderer took to paved streets and the trail was lost.

It appeared the murderer was well versed in crime. Following the shooting he calmly walked across the street and began talking with Charles Rowett, who had come out of his house when he heard the shots. Realizing he was talking to a person who had a gun in his hands, Rowett tried to apprehend the criminal who ran down the street firing one bullet at Rowett.

There were two differing descriptions of the murderer. Mrs. Borden claimed she had seen a young man carrying a lamp from one of the rear rooms of the burglarized house, while Mr. Rowett swore the man who fired at him was about 50 years of age. This led to the theory that there were two perpetrators and that they were the pair who slugged and nearly killed W.A. Alston at his Pike theater the previous week. Within a short time Police Chief Moyer had men stationed at all the Pacific Electric and railway stations leading to Los Angeles and Orange

County. His department notified the police of every nearby city, and assigned officers to search every rooming house in Long Beach in hopes of gaining some tangible clue that would lead to solving the murder.

The city was stunned by this tragedy. Borden was one of the oldest members of the Police Department and well loved by everyone. The flag over City Hall was lowered to half mast in honor of the slain police officer. The mayor quickly announced a $1,000 reward for information leading to the arrest and conviction of the murderer.

Borden's roots in the city went deep. He had built the first house in what was to become Long Beach in 1879. Leasing land from Jotham Bixby, the Bordens, who resided in Downey the rest of the year, lived in the little house during sowing and harvesting season. It was the only dwelling between the Los Cerritos ranch house (still standing at 4600 N. Virginia Road) and the sea. After the harvest flocks of Bixby sheep were allowed to roam over the acreage and the house was used as a sheepherder's cottage. In 1901 Tom Borden, his wife and five children (Archy, Ella, Josie, Tillie and Tommie) returned to Long Beach to make this their permanent home. Tom had had enough of farming and decided to join the mounted police force.

It seemed the police had Borden's killer when William Davies was arrested and identified by Mrs. Borden as being the intruder she had seen in her house the evening of the murder. However, Davies had an alibi and was soon released. Later, former San Quentin inmate Joseph E. Jones was acknowledged as the killer. He had been identified from a police photo taken when he was sent to prison for burglary. Hearing that the police were out to arrest him, Jones escaped by boarding an electric Red Car to Los Angeles. He disappeared, and later was reported to have died in another part of the country. But had he really killed Borden? And what about the theory that two men had been involved? Both questions remain unanswered to this day.

The death of police officer Borden severely upset his colleagues and residents. Everyone was on edge. Could it happen again? As nerves intensified, tragedy struck again. Patrolman Ralph Powell shot and wounded an innocent African American he mistook as a burglar.

On March 22, 1912, five days after the Borden murder, Sam Thomas went to visit his fiancée, Maude Gibson, who worked for the Vandewater family in an affluent part of Long Beach. Waiting for her to get off work, Sam took out a cigarette and was strolling back and forth in front of the house when a neighbor panicked. Because Sam was a black man in a white neighborhood he was mistaken for a criminal. Neighbors called the police reporting a prowler in the area. Powell, jumpy because of Borden's death, shot first and asked questions later. It was clearly a result of police negligence but understandable, most people thought, considering the circumstances.

For eight weeks after he was injured Sam Thomas lived at the home of friends, with the city contributing $10/week for his care. At the end of two months, and showing little improvement, Sam was taken to the county hospital where he was operated on and where he remained a charity case, unassisted by the city. On January 30, 1914, Sam was released from the hospital and once again came to Long Beach, residing with friends. His left arm was disabled, his left leg partially paralyzed and his overall health poor.

Laws of the time barred Sam from any financial relief from the city, even though the city was morally responsible because Sam was injured by a city policeman. He tried to sue Officer Powell, but lost. This formerly big, husky fellow, who had served in the Spanish American war, now had to subsist on meager charitable donations.

The City Council believed they had a moral obligation to provide Sam Thomas a means for earning a livelihood. Various state laws forbid the city from putting him on a regular pension-type income. All that Long Beach could legally do was provide him with a job. In August 1914 they appointed him city hall janitor at a salary of $35 a month. They had to dismiss the former janitor, another African American named Levi Howard, from the position. The *Long Beach Press* expressed the feelings of the city:

"Maybe it's a trifle tough on Howard, but he can easily find another job and the city is in no manner beholden to him. Anyway, Sam Thomas, colored, is janitor of the city hall, Levi Howard, colored, is relieved of the position." (LB Press 8/1/1914)

By strange coincidence Police Sergeant Powell, who shot Sam Thomas by accident, also became a cripple, having been critically injured in a traffic accident in performance of his duties. This was in the days before pensions and public relief. It did not matter that Powell was physically disabled in the course of his job as a police officer. Cities did not have to legally provide for employees hurt while doing the jobs they were paid for. The city did, however, allow Ralph Powell to remain on the police force as a clerk.

Some good did come out of all of this. Police Sergeant Fred Kutz decided that the department needed up-to-date technology and equipment if it was to solve Borden's murder and future crimes. At his own expense he installed a fingerprinting system, learning the techniques needed to utilize this new state-of-the art system.

Sir Francis Galton, a British anthropologist and a cousin of Charles Darwin, began to realize that fingerprints could be used as a unique means of identification in the 1880's. In 1892 he published his findings in a book, *Fingerprint*. In it he also established a fingerprint classification system. The U.S. Army began using Galton's system in

1905. Two years later the U.S. Navy started, followed shortly thereafter by the Marine Corps. During the next 25 years more and more law enforcement agencies joined in the use of fingerprints as a means of personal identification. Many of these agencies began sending copies of their fingerprint cards to the National Bureau of Criminal Identification, which was established by the International Association of Police Chiefs. In Long Beach the first important identification made by Long Beach police as a result of fingerprinting was that of William Van Boyer, arrested for burglarizing an Edison Company employee's locker. His fingerprints sent him back to Folsom prison.

Thirteen months after Borden's murder the Long Beach Police Department had a total of 241 fingerprints on file: 206 from outside sources and 35 made by the department itself. The police officer's killing was the trigger leading towards the modern crime scene investigation techniques Long Beach utilizes today.

Death not Staged

Ah, vaudeville. Long Beach folk loved this low cost form of entertainment which appealed to the young and old of either gender. From the early 1880's to the 1930's vaudeville was one of the most popular kinds of amusement in America. Types of acts included musicians (both classical and popular), dancers, comedians, trained animals, magicians, female and male impersonators, acrobats, one-act plays or scenes from plays, lecturing celebrities, minstrels, and short movies. It was a family kind of place, generally alcohol free, espousing Christian values and good, clean fun.

In Long Beach folks flocked to the Byde-a-Wyle Theater on the Pike. It was one of the most popular vaudeville houses in town. Comedian Roscoe "Fatty" Arbuckle, who would go on to silent picture fame and sadly be most remembered for a heavily publicized criminal prosecution that ended his career, got his start at the Byde-a-Wyle. In 1908 he married Minta Durfee, a fellow comedian, on the stage of the theater.

Not all theater couples were as happy as Minta and Fatty during their early years. On the morning of August 22, 1909, Albert F. Roth, shot and killed himself in the corridor of Long Beach's Hotel del Mar in front of the apartment of actress Daisy Cort, a performer at the Byde-a-Wyle.

Hotel guests were roused from their sleep at 6:30 a.m. when they heard the sound of a pistol shot echoing through the hallways of the hotel. Hurrying down the corridor to see what had happened, they found the body of a man in front of room 65. His hat had fallen over his face and his fingers still clutched the trigger of the revolver. The bullet had entered his skull at his right temple. Death was instantaneous. While the first guest bent over the man on the floor, the door of room 65 opened and Miss Cort peered outside. As she glanced at the body she screamed, "My God, I believe that is my husband!" She was right.

It seemed that Albert Roth had staked out the theater and the hotel hoping to catch his wife with another man. A few days earlier he had been talking to another actress, a Miss Gores, and intimated that he intended to kill his wife and then himself. The young actress had told him to forget such a dreadful idea and instead concentrate on winning back his wife's affections. But Roth continued to follow Daisy, who was out late with friends the night of his suicide. Whether he intended to kill his wife and then himself was not known, but Daisy Cort hadn't heard a sound until aroused by the shot.

In a band of Roth's hat a note addressed to Mr. Bartow, proprietor of the hotel, was found. On the opposite page was a note to his wife. The note to Bartow read:

"Notify my wife, Daisy Cort, room 65. Mr. Bartow, I am sorry to do this in your hotel, but I could not stand it any longer."

The note to his wife read:

"Laura, dear, I could not stand it any longer. I watched you tonight and you seemed to be full of fun, not giving me a thought. Kindly do what you can in the way of sending my body to Chicago and forgive me for I

love you so much. Your clothes are in my trunk and the black dress is at the tailors."

In his coat pocket were two addressed letters, one to D. Friedl and another to Mrs. A. Trunk both of Chicago. The letter to Friedl read:

"Dear parents: When you receive this note, I will be no more. Laura has caused me to do it. Please forgive me, but life was not worth living without her."

The letter to Mrs. Trunk read:

"Dear Bella and Ma: when you receive this I will be no more. Laura caused me to do it and I could not stand it any longer. She ran around with other men and stayed away from her hotel all night and I could not see her fall so low."(LA Times 8/23/1909)

Other letters, written by his wife from various cities in which she performed, were also found in his possession. All were loving, except the last, written from San Bernardino. In it Daisy asked Roth not to think her harsh, but to keep his nose out of her business. Friends of Daisy Cort aka Laura Roth said she had been worried about her husband because he didn't want to work, expecting his wife to support him. Lately he had been trying to pose as her manager and, as such, get her salary, which she resented. Upon further questioning she revealed some surprising information about her dead husband.

It seemed the couple had first met in Chicago, where Daisy/Laura was a chorus girl. In 1904 they married and she discovered her husband's real name was Anton F. Friedl. But Anton was a fugitive from justice, wanted in Chicago for embezzlement. He promised her he had reformed, but he thought it best to take on her maiden name, Roth. He came to Los Angeles in January 1909 and she followed two months later. For a time they were happy together but when she discovered Roth had passed some bad checks she was convinced he hadn't changed. She wanted nothing more to do with him. He continued to follow her and made threats against her life. Fortunately he had not followed his original plan of killing his wife, then himself.

What happened to Daisy/Laura? She seems to have disappeared from the theater circuit. Perhaps, like so many others with a past she hoped to forget, she once again changed her name and went on to become a star in the newest form of entertainment, motion pictures.

Marry Me or Die

In 1910 tongues in Long Beach were wagging over the affairs of millionaire mine owner Alva D. Myers whose home on Ocean Avenue was the costliest in the city. "Goldfield Al" Myers made an enormous fortune during the gold rush days. Starting off with nothing but a burro, a side of bacon, a coffee pot, a pick and a pan, his worth in 1910 was estimated to be between 3 to 10 million dollars. His home reflected his wealth. All the hardware, including door hinges and knobs were gold plated by a Los Angeles jewelry firm, leading many to believe the door knobs were solid gold. He even had a swimming pool built in the basement of the house. Concrete steps led to the level of the beach below and there was a special bathhouse for ocean bathing. Only the finest and highest grade materials were used in Myers' mansion. In 1908 people were amazed to read that Myers was also building an "auto home" for his automobile. The estimated cost for this garage was $5,750—this was double the amount required to build a good two story frame residence at the time.

Myers and his wife Mattie began building their $225,000 home at 1800 E. Ocean in 1907. The couple had married March 9, 1906. Soon after saying "I do," Mattie found that Al became violent when he drank. The last straw was when Myers fired a shot at her in their not yet fully completed mansion in Long Beach. In May 1909 she secured a divorce from Myers, receiving between $75,000 and $100,000 as her share of the community property. Women problems continued to plague Myers. In October 1910 Miss Julia Ward Gibson drew a revolver and threatened to shoot him unless he married her.

The October 13, 1910, issue of the *Daily Telegram* told the story. It quoted Julia Ward as saying: "After I had drawn the revolver, I found that I had not the heart to kill the man I love more than life itself." Miss Gibson had also brought along her father, a retired Presbyterian minister, to perform the wedding ceremony. She had obtained a marriage license that same afternoon and was sure, with the help of a pistol, she could get Myers to marry her. Seeing the gun in the hands of the excited young woman, Myers made a bee line for the dining room where he armed himself with a thirty-two automatic. He called his housekeeper on a private phone and asked her to summon the police. When the police arrived Miss Gibson quietly handed over the gun.

The circumstances leading up to this sensational episode began in June 1909. Miss Gibson, a writer of some note, asked Myers for permission to visit his home and interview him for a story she was writing. Myers agreed, and this visit led to others. Letters were written, marriage was promised. In February 1910 Miss Gibson brought a $100,000 suit against Myers for seduction and breach of promise, but she had a change of heart. In August Julia Gibson began telephoning Myers daily, telling him she was withdrawing the suit and asking him to resume their relationship and marry her. Myers refused and told her to go ahead with the lawsuit. Miss Gibson told a different tale. She said she and Myers were becoming chummy again and when she heard Myers planned to marry another woman she was forced to act.

Julia was arrested for this well publicized attempted murder. Her notoriety followed her. While in prison awaiting trial she received flowers, boxes of candy and other gifts from another admirer who Julia identified only as a prominent Los Angeles real estate operator. But Julia told the press that she loved only Myers and would keep on loving him because "woman is so constituted." *(LA Times* 10/16/1910). In an attempt to end the matter quickly, Goldfield Al declined to press charges asking only that Miss Gibson give him no further trouble.

In 1911 Myers, anxious to escape the notoriety and Miss Gibson, sold his home to Jotham Bixby who purchased it as a 50th wedding anniversary gift for his wife. Myers took a financial loss, selling the $225,000 home for $75,000 cash. He moved to Nevada devoting most of his time and energy to his mines. He eventually returned to Long Beach in 1912 and wed again. His bride was Hedwig Jablonski, the daughter of a Berlin banker. Thirteen weeks earlier they had met on a train coming from Chicago to Long Beach. They were married in Myers' sister's home in Carroll Park.

Myers, who lost most of his fortune during the Nevada bank failures in 1927, became a semi-invalid from injuries received in an automobile accident in 1937. He died October 16, 1949, at the age of 77. He had, however, out-lasted his extraordinary house, which was destroyed by the 1933 Long Beach earthquake.

Murder Country Style

It's hard for us living in the 21st century to imagine Long Beach as being mainly farm land, but that's the way it was up through World War II. Agriculture was the major source of income, with tourism and the various summer gatherings a distant second. In 1895, for instance, land sold from $65 to $200 per acre, depending on location. Most of the new farmers had to find outside employment for a year or two before their crops began to pay off. But Long Beach land was fertile. Locals said if a man had a horse, wagon and cultivating implements, he could, by crop rotation and proper irrigation, produce more on ten acres of Long Beach land than on forty acres east of the Rockies. Smart land usage counted for a lot. For instance, if a farmer planted fruit trees over most of his land, vegetables and berries could be raised between the rows of trees for the first two or three years.

A successful farmer had to watch his markets and anticipate what produce would be needed most and when. This way he could bring in a larger return on his investment. He also had to be frugal, recycling everything into compost to be used as fertilizer. Trips to town also had to serve a dual purpose, when a load of produce was taken to market, a load of plant food or supplies brought back.

But farmers also needed more than just compost to make their crops grow. Nothing worked better than good old fashioned animal droppings. Many turned to cantankerous "Old Man" Ranous, a manure dealer, who lived in a shack at the corner of Fifteenth and Walnut.

Customers became worried when seventy-year-old Ranous, a widower, disappeared September 21, 1910, leaving behind his unfed animals and his walking stick, which he never went anywhere without. When last seen, the Civil War veteran was wearing a sweater, slouch hat and overalls. His Mexican helper, Sam Apodaco, said Ranous was planning a trip into Los Angeles that day to file a civil suit against his son-in-law Steve DeVoe, who Ranous believed was embezzling from him. Ranous had never liked his son-in-law, friends testified. In fact, many remembered him rushing to Santa Ana in 1896 trying to stop the marriage of his 18-year-old daughter, Rosa Pearl, to 33-year-old DeVoe. Ranous' disappearance seemed like foul play, but nothing could be done without a body.

Business went on and customers became used to helping themselves, leaving money with Apodaco for Ranous when, hopefully, he returned. On October 27th Ranous did return, in a way. A Japanese customer was getting some manure when his shovel brought up a moldering human leg from the depths of the manure pile. The clothes, which identified the corpse as Ranous, had been preserved, but the corpse itself was almost totally decomposed. The body had originally been placed on about six inches of manure and covered over with more than a wagon load of the same. Curiously, the pile had been searched for a sign of a body several weeks prior to this grisly find, but it was DeVoe, Ranous' son-in-law, who had done the searching. Steve DeVoe was arrested on suspicion of murder.

Yet DeVoe was not the only one under suspicion. The Mexican worker, Apodaco, had also been seen arguing with Ranous. Neighbors reported hearing shots at the Ranous shack on the evening of September 21st. Upon investigation, Long Beach police chief Clarence E. Moyer discovered Apodaco had bought a revolver from a Los Angeles pawnbroker on September 21st and returned it the next day claiming the revolver would not work properly. Chief Moyer said one chamber of the revolver had been emptied while in Apodaco's possession. There was other evidence which pointed to Apodaco. He had stopped working after Ranous disappeared, acting like he knew his employer would not return. He also went on spending sprees, with more money than he could possibly have earned. He also attempted to sell Ranous' horses and ducks before the body was discovered.

Ranous had not been an easy fellow to get along with. There were reports in the newspapers about his run-ins with the law going back as far as 1903. He argued with many, usually over money matters. Sometimes he was so vociferous in his accusations that he was arrested for disturbing the peace. Even though he was not a likable fellow everyone agreed that he had not deserved this kind of death.

Dr. Bishop, in the post-mortem examination reported in the October 29th edition of the *Daily Telegram*, discovered a wound in the manure ridden skull which he believed had killed the aged man. The hole had been made by some heavy instrument of iron or other hard substance and broke through the outer shell of bone covering the back of the head just above the base of the skull. This, Dr. Bishop believed, was sufficient to cause instant death.

No gunshot wound could be found on the badly decomposed cadaver. The police investigators even severed the head from the body and boiled it, looking for signs of a bullet. Bishop made a through search of the skull, but found neither a bullet nor any trace of where a bullet had entered the head. "There was no bullet marks on the body, as far as I can find," he said. "Of course there's the possibility there might have been a bullet fired through the neck. No trace of a bullet wound could be found in the flesh, owing to the condition of the body."

On April 4, 1911, Sam Apodaco was convicted of murdering James S. Ranous and sentenced to ten years in San Quentin.

One of the farms that provided Ranous with manure was the Torrey dairy farm, five miles northwest of Long Beach. Tragedy and murder had also occurred here on September 9, 1906, when 17-year-old Constance Lilley shot and killed his 18-year-old roommate Alex Gonzales.

During morning milking two shots were heard and farmhands hurried towards the sound. They found Gonzales lying on his face a bullet just under the right ear, another through his back. Near him stood Lilley, white and trembling, with a revolver in his hand. He turned and faced them saying: "I got him that time; he'll bother me no more." (*Daily Telegram* 9/10/1906). While the others were busy trying to revive Gonzales, Lilley disappeared. He had gone home to mom.

Following the long walk home, Lilley told his mother everything. She advised him to give himself up. Not wanting to disappoint her, he agreed. She may have had her doubts that her son would follow her advice for she insisted he take his little sister along. On board the Pacific Electric heading to Long Beach, Lilley told his sister he suddenly remembered he had left his watch and money at Torrey's ranch. He sent his sister home, telling her he'd go to the police as soon as he retrieved his things from the farm. He then disappeared.

Word of the murder had already reached Long Beach. Police went searching for Lilley at his mother's house and were taken aback when she told them her son had gone to town to surrender. But where was he? A police bulletin was sent out and Lilley was spotted traveling to Santa Ana on a bicycle. With the help of the Santa Ana police, Lilley was apprehended. "My father will see me through," Lilley said to *Daily*

Telegram reporters. "I have plenty of witnesses to prove that I was molested by the Greaser and threatened."

But Robert Gunnison, a foreman on the Torrey ranch, told a different story. He said he had heard the boys quarrelling a few days earlier. He went to break them up and Gonzales told him Lilley had drawn a knife on him. Lilley had refused to discuss the matter. He said nothing, just walked away, going to dinner. As Lilley strolled towards the cook house Gunnison did notice that the teenager kept his right hand in his hip pocket where, Gunnison surmised, he had a revolver.

The morning of the murder Gunnison and Mr. Torrey were in the barn getting some hay. Suddenly they heard two shots fired in quick succession. As they rushed to the scene they saw Lilley walking about, looking like he had nothing to do with the shooting. However, the smoking revolver he carried in his hand gave him away. Lilley told the men that Gonzales had threatened him with a club, but when Gunnison and Torrey looked around they found no club. They also knew for a fact that young Gonzales never carried a revolver.

At the trial Gunnison stated that Lilley's parents were divorced and Lilley had recently visited his father in Pendleton, Oregon. Lilley came back certain his dad would defend him if he ever got into any trouble. Gunnison believed Lilley wanted to make a name for himself as a gun fighter. He seemed to have a mean streak in him and was sickly obsessed with guns. In fact, Lilley had deliberately shot a dog to death soon after he went to work on the ranch. Also, when told to kill a sick calf mercifully by knocking it in the head, Lilly had tied it to a tree and amused himself by shooting at it with a small caliber Winchester. He fired twelve shots before the tortured animal died.

Lilley showed no interest in his trial, a bored look etched across his face. After all, wasn't this the way a cool gunfighter would act if on trial for murder? Lilley didn't even flinch when Torrey, overcome by emotion, broke down in tears as he described Gonzales' life. The only visible sign of emotion, the *Daily Telegram* reported, was the intense hatred which gleamed from Lilley's half closed eyes when Gunnison told what he knew of the relations between the two boys.

When Lilley testified he spoke coolly, never raising his eyes. He refused to give any detailed statement, confining himself to simple responses to questions put to him. He did reveal a criminal side to Gonzales that few believed. He said Gonzales proposed that they hold up a neighbor some night and when he refused Gonzales had threatened his life. On the morning of the shooting, after the milking had been done, Lilley said he went to see if all the cows had been milked, and found one that had not. He told Gonzales to milk the cow and Gonzales replied he'd do it that afternoon. Lilley objected and Gonzales struck him. Lilley then drew his pistol and shot his roommate twice. Lilley claimed he was afraid for his life and thought Gonzales had a knife. He asserted he had seen Gonzales with two corn knives which he kept in their room.

Lilley's unruffled demeanor changed when the verdict was read. He visibly wept when the sentence was handed down. He had expected a verdict of self defense, but he should have been happy. He could have been given a death sentence, but because of his young age he was instead sentenced to six years in prison.

Alex Gonzales' body lay unclaimed. No relatives could be found. He was buried in potter's field at the Municipal Cemetery.

Lover's triangle?

On January 17, 1911, a 24-year-old Englishman, George Richard Ward, shot and killed 44-year-old John Bowers at Bowers' pretty bungalow on the Long Beach bluff. Death was instantaneous, and the only witness the slayer, George Richard Ward. Speculation raged. Was it a lover's triangle? Was Ward romantically linked to Mrs. Nellie Bowers, a 34-year-old beauty?

John Bowers had met his wife in London, England. As a young man Bowers had left his home in Minnesota to study photography, eventually opening studios in London, Paris, Washington and Pretoria, South Africa. While in England he fell in love and married Ellen "Nellie" Bygott. They had two children, 13-year-old Queenie and 5-year-old Walter. The couple knew Ward in England and later met him again in South Africa. When Bowers returned to America with his family they continued to correspond with Ward. In December 1910 Ward joined them in Long Beach. Having no job and little money, John Bowers invited Ward to make his home with them until he found employment.

When interviewed about the tragedy Ward claimed Bowers had supposedly left for a three day trip the day he was shot. The night of the shooting, Mrs. Bowers testified, she had attended a meeting of the Order of the Eastern Star, and when the session lasted longer than usual she telephoned home and asked Ward to come downtown and act as her escort home. Nearing the Bowers' residence at 1372 E. Ocean, both noticed a strange man prowling around the place. The stranger ran away when the pair called out to him. This incident made Mrs. Bowers nervous and, at her invitation (also verified by her brother-in-law, Thomas Bowers, who was also a guest in the house), a couch was arranged for Ward so that he could sleep inside that night and not in the guest house. Ward claimed he was awakened by a noise about 2 o'clock. As he opened the door to find out what was happening, he was confronted by a masked man. The man jumped toward him when Ward demanded the stranger's name. Ward then fired the fatal shot. As the man fell, Ward raised the man's mask and discovered to his horror that he had killed his friend John Bowers. Ward shouted for help and Nellie Bowers came running. Together the couple went to awaken Tom Bowers, who was almost deaf. Jointly the three carried the body into the house. Ward ran for a doctor, and told him he had mistaken Bowers for a burglar and killed him.

George Richard Ward was arrested for manslaughter, but the charge was later changed to murder. With the manslaughter charge the district attorney's office would have to prove beyond a doubt that the killing was willful and with malice. The prosecution now only had to prove that the killing occurred, and the defendant prove there was no malice or aforethought in the sad tragedy.

Why was Bowers prowling around his own house dressed in his Japanese assistant's clothing so late at night? In the right hand pocket of Bowers' pants was a loaded revolver and a nearly-full box of cartridges. Was he trying to catch Ward and Nellie in a compromising situation? Nellie did testify that Bowers was very jealous of her.

Bowers' partner, I. Asai, cleared up a few details. Asai left with Bowers the afternoon before the murder for Los Angeles; from there

Bowers was to go to Oceanside and Asai to Santa Paula to collect accounts due them. Before they parted Bowers cashed a check for $5, and with this money probably purchased the gun found upon his dead body. Asai identified the green hat and black strips of cloth as his own, and said they were in his room when he left. Asai revealed that Bowers had been down in the dumps for several days, but Asai thought it was because business was slow. Though John and Nellie Bowers sometimes quarreled, Bowers had never said anything to Asai which suggested jealousy over Ward. In fact Bowers seemed to pity Ward because of his poor health.

Nellie Bowers' testimony did not waver. She agreed with the story both she and Ward had given the police. Under pressure, she did finally admit to having a recent affair with a Long Beach actor, which could have aroused her husband's suspicions. When Ward was called to the stand, his story stood pat. He said that after living in Africa he was used to carrying a gun around. He said he simply exercised the right of every man to protect himself and the home he was in.

The prosecution tried to prove that Ward must have known the man he was shooting was John Bowers. It had been the night of a full moon with light as intense as that of a street lamp. An affair between Ward and Nellie Bowers was alluded to and the heartless and unnatural way Nellie left her husband's dead body crumpled up on the steps. A loving wife would have stayed with her spouse, cradling him in her arms as he lay dying, the prosecution asserted. Ward could have gone alone to awaken Tom Bowers. After thirty ballots and sixteen hours of debate the jury could not come to a verdict. Four stood for conviction, eight for acquittal. A new trial was set for May 8, 1911.

A pale but composed George Richard Ward appeared in court that day expecting to recount and relive the tragedy once again. However, the deputy district attorney said that because the former evidence was insufficient and no new evidence had come to light to strengthen the state's case, he asked that the case be dismissed. Ward, after four months confinement, stepped from the court room a free man.

The Bowers' home on East Ocean became a tourist attraction for amateur sleuths wandering around the premises, discussing the case. The favorite pastime of the visitors was looking for blood stains. Not only did they search on the wooden front porch where the body of Bowers was said to have been found, but the lawn, under bushes and up and down the wooden steps to the strand below the bluff. They were looking for clues to find out what had really happened. Had Nellie Bowers and Ward been telling the truth? The court thought so, because there was no evidence to prove otherwise. Eventually rain washed away the blood and the ghoulish amateur detectives gradually lost interest. Ironically, Bowers continued to provide for his family even after his death. Nearly a year after his demise, Bowers was granted a patent on a new photographic device which, when sold, brought money to the still grieving children.

Baby Goodbyes

It was hard for most to believe, and generally kept quiet. If word got out the reputation of the city would be tarnished. Who would believe that dead babies were sometimes found abandoned in various locations throughout Long Beach? But word leaked out and the press picked up the stories.

On March 7, 1916, Joseph Flacy, a carpenter, entered a vacant house at 331 E. 16th Street and found the dead body of an infant. It was partially decomposed and had probably been there for at least a month. It appeared to have died within a few hours of its birth. Amazingly, the dead body of another baby was found wrapped in rags and paper inside a little wooden box on the slimy bank of the Cerritos slough under the Seventh Street Bridge that same day. The corpse was of a white male, with black curly hair, born alive but then apparently suffocated. Another uncanny coincidence was that at that same place, under the bridge, another dead body of a newborn Mexican baby boy, similarly clothed, had been found four years earlier.

Another tragic discovery was made by L.M. Jacobs while canvassing the harbor industrial district looking for a job. He found a wrapped-up, soaking wet package just at the shore's edge. Evidently the parcel had been thrown into the water. As the tide receded the bundle had been deposited upon the muddy beach. Jacobs thought he had found something valuable, but when he untied the gunnysack he found the wooden crate and an infant's corpse. Not long afterwards, on March 9, 1918, the body of a ten-pound infant boy was found on the beach near the municipal band stand. Covered with a black silk automobile cover and wrapped in newspaper, the child had apparently met its death by drowning. The city health officer believed both babies to be less than a week old when discarded. Both had been born alive and normal.

Evidently, some mothers had qualms about murdering their unwanted infants. On July 12, 1917, Civil War veteran Hiram Dane found a perfectly healthy brown-eyed baby, less than a month old, abandoned near the city incinerator. Would the baby have died if Dane hadn't found him? Had the mother been about to toss her child into the incinerator (and burn all evidence of his existence), before she had a change of heart? Was she watching nearby to assure her baby was found by a loving soul?

Mother love is supposedly one of the most powerful forces in nature. What could cause a mother to commit such inhumane actions? Had the unwanted pregnancies been a result of rape? Or perhaps the women were prostitutes? It made little difference. Annie W. Allen in an article entitled "How to Save Girls Who Have Fallen" published in *Survey* August 6, 1910, expressed the general view of the time:

"A girl must remain a virgin until she becomes a wife. She must be made to abhor any other thought. She must realize that if she does not remain pure, she is no longer in the company of valuable women. She has fallen and become unfit for her proper uses, unfit for honor and praise. The race could never have advanced without this belief. It is absolutely essential to our life. It is herein absolutely right."

The Bethlehem Inn at 27 Maine Avenue opened in 1909 to help prevent such tragedies. For some time a group of Long Beach women had been planning a maternity home to which pregnant women could come. The purpose of the organization stated:

"The Bethlehem Inn Association has been organized by women of Long Beach, as an approved home for poor, needy, friendless, destitute, homeless or temporarily embarrassed." (Long Beach Sun 9/5/1933).

Membership dues in the association were $1 a year, and neither salaries nor rents were paid from hospital funds. All furnishings of the Inn were donated, including the three beds; funds were solicited from banks, clubs and business firms. Mrs. Charles Healey, who was in charge of finances, later told *Long Beach Sun* readers that nearly everyone paid something, whatever they could, and if impossible to pay in money service was contributed. No discrimination was made between paying patients and those who could not pay. However, she neglected to say in the retrospective 1933 article, only married women need apply.

Seeing the plight of unmarried, pregnant women Dr. W. Harriman Jones, a prominent Long Beach physician, refused to continue financially supporting the Bethlehem Inn. He, and many other contributors, felt the maternity hospital should admit all patients, even if they couldn't show a marriage license at the door.

On January 28, 1915, the hospital association decided to give up the maternity hospital rather than surrender their cherished principle of "no marriage license, no admission." Others said the Bethlehem Inn should have changed its name for it was most un-like Christ, who forgave Mary Magdalen.

Life was stressful for many Long Beach women. Unwanted pregnancies added to their woes, especially if the mother believed the father of the baby was not her husband. Such was the case of Caroline Raab.

The summer of 1914 was full of dreadful stories of floods, volcanoes and war. Here in Long Beach people were still recovering from one of the worst gales in city history. Trees and telegraph poles were leveled that February, railroad connections cut off and telephone service crippled. In June Mount Lassen in Northern California erupted, marking a year long period of volcanic activity. The Mexican revolution continued to rage throughout the year and rumors of U.S. intervention caused our local National Guard unit, Company H, to prepare for war. Turmoil also exploded onto the scene—on August 1, 1914, Germany declared war in Europe.

All of this unrest, especially in Europe, was stressful to German immigrants Fred and Caroline Raab who had many family members living in Germany. They worried that war would break out and many whom they loved would die. Fortunately for Caroline she would not have to hear of Germany's declaration of war. She would be dead.

On June 3, 1914, twenty-nine-year-old Caroline Raab locked her 3-year-old-son out of the house and then proceeded to cut the throats of her two young daughters and herself with a razor. She felt her son, as a male, had a much better life to look forward to than her daughters.

The little girls were playing in the yard at 1384 Redondo Avenue with their brother Fritz. When their mother called the girls to come into the home, the young boy ran after them, but the mother locked the front door. He went to the back door and found it was also locked. Meanwhile the crazed mother was at her fatal work. When young Fritz heard the cries of his mother and sisters he began to cry. Neighbors saw the little fellow sobbing and, investigating, came across the grisly scene.

The mother, a deep gash at her throat, lay across the head of the bed with 18-month-old Lillian at her side. Lillian lay on her mother's right arm, the baby's head nearly severed. Lena, aged 5, lay partly under the bed in a deep pool of blood, several deep gashes on her throat. The blade of a razor was found on the floor, and the handle under Mrs. Raab's body.

Upon hearing of the tragedy Fred Raab, who ran a small upholstering shop, rushed home. Though friends attempted to restrain him, he burst into the room and threw himself on the bodies of his loved ones. Police had to use force to get him away from the scene. Between sobs Raab told the following story:

"My wife had female trouble for years. In January I told her to go to Dr. Hill. She went to the physician several times. In February she made a confession to me which made my blood boil, and I went to attorney Roland Swaffield about it." (LA Times 6/4/1914)

Swaffield confirmed Raab's story. He said Raab told him he didn't want to get a divorce, but he would like to send his wife back to Germany and also kill Dr. Hill. Dr. Hill, it seemed, had "taken advantage" of Caroline during her visits and she was now pregnant with his child. The attorney advised Raab that nothing could be proved, for him to go home, patch up the trouble, and perhaps later move out of town. That was the last time Swaffield had seen Raab.

That was not the end of the evidence. Mrs. Raab left a note behind, written in German. Once translated, it sent shockwaves throughout the community. It read:

"*Love, good-by. My dear good Fritz and papa. Once more, for the last time, dear child, I was not to blame for it. Those who have done this to me and our beautiful family may regret it, but it is too late now. I am not alone who is to suffer innocently, Dear Fritz and papa. If you had only told me the truth. I hope that they will console you for what has been brought over us. Don't forget the beautiful, happy days we have had before I got into the hands of that man. Although I was homesick, we were happy anyway. I know that you always meant well. I wish you much luck in your progress but it hurts, dear Fred. Be a good papa to Fritz. I wish you all the luck. Once more, my best to those which worked so hard on this. I hardly believe it will bring them much luck. I don't call that sympathy. Don't forget how precious I got along with everything before I got in the hands of that man Hill.*

I am convinced that there are still some who think and know that I am innocent. I am sorry to say that this man had his control over me. Let my dear parents and brothers and sisters know at once. I bid them a thousand times good-by. I hope that they will not worry too much over it, but you were foolish enough that you believed those in San Diego more than me. I would very much like to see you once more, but sorry. God bless you; it could have been so nice. God bless you, it was not to be. My heart belongs to you. Is there any better child than you? It is too bad that you let them persuade you.

Send my dearest mama a souvenir of me. Assure her that I was not to blame for it. I hope that those who ruined me will console you. If you have anything to give away of my possessions, don't give anything to this neighborhood, and tell certain ones to mind their own business as they will have just enough to do then. It is not for my sake but for our dearest children, and for yourself, poor, poor Fred. How I would like to see you once more. Forget, dear papa. I wish you luck a thousand times more. You know I love you unto death, and keep up courage and control yourself and don't get discouraged. You will find our dear little children again. I am sorry that

I have no chance to see you any more. Farewell, my dear child, and Fritzie. Don't get discouraged. Good-by until I see you again.

P.S. The child which I expect is from Dr. Hill." (Daily Telegram 6/4/1914)

An autopsy did show she was three and a half months pregnant. But who was the father?

Dr. Hill, though arrested, avowed the accusations were from a mentally ill woman whom he had been treating for a "nervous condition." The physicians of Long Beach and members of the First Methodist Episcopal Church quickly signed statements expressing their full confidence in Dr. Hill's innocence. On June 5, 1914, Dr. Walter Hill was released by the police and exonerated from all blame. A coroner's jury rendered a simple verdict of suicide.

Raab stated he was not yet done with Dr. Hill. He knew Hill's wife was an invalid, possibly unable to perform her "wifely duties." His wife was young and beautiful, spoke little English and would have been the perfect candidate for the doctor's seduction. However Raab's business was poor, he could not afford to leave town or pay an attorney. He also had a son to support. He pursued the matter no further.

Dr. Hill later had a Long Beach school named for him.

Another mother took her own life and that of her 7-year-old son on January 22, 1917. Finances and poor health were the probable causes, though a naïve second husband, who thought a kiss could cure his wife's depression, thought otherwise.

Charles Smith told authorities he had hurriedly left for work that morning forgetting, for the first time since their marriage six months earlier, to kiss his wife goodbye. When he returned to their home at 616 Lime later that evening her found her and her son from a previous marriage together in bed, dead. They had ended their lives by inhaling gas from a tube extending from the wall furnace to the bed. A towel was drawn over their heads. The 35-year-old mother was still holding her son in her arms, while the tube between them still hissed forth its deadly fumes.

Charles Smith could not stop thinking that his failure to kiss his wife goodbye might have been the direct cause for her act. He did admit, however, that their finances had taken a turn for the worse and Mrs. Smith had been troubled with bad health for some time. She had been listless and depressed and had threatened before to end her life. He had always cheered her up by telling her how much he loved her, but he had forgotten to express his devotion to her that morning.

Could lack of a kiss have led to Mrs. Smith's suicide and murder of her son, or was Charles Smith just trying to assuage his guilt over not seeking medical treatment for his severely depressed new wife? It was a question only he could answer and live with.

Death to Love

"No girl should be allowed to be on the street alone, day or night," Mrs. F.E. Young, president of the Long Beach federation of the Women's Christian Temperance Union said in August 1913. She warned young ladies to be aware of the traffic in prostitution and the possibility they might be kidnapped by white slavers.

The National Welfare League had received word through unnamed sources that white slave dealers had been asked to furnish 2,000 girls from the Pacific coast during the Panama-Pacific Exposition at San Francisco and San Diego the following year. What the white slavers did was lure unsuspecting young women into a situation where they would be drugged and raped. Their reputations would be soiled and they would have nowhere to turn except to prostitution. Since July 25th several girls had disappeared from Venice, California. The league warned that no girl was safe unless she had a trustworthy escort.

Mrs. Young told the story of one Poly High School miss who had a narrow escape from a scheming madam who was posing as a deaconess in the Nazarene Church in Long Beach. The teenager had gone to a mission meeting at the church while her parents were vacationing in the east. She became so concerned about the Africans in Africa, who had not heard of Christianity, that she decided she had a calling to become a missionary. The deaconess told the girl that she could go to Africa with her, but first they would go to San Francisco to catch a ship.

When the mother returned, her daughter told her of her plans. The older woman expressed concerns but the girl refused to listen, certain she was being guided in her course of action by God. The mother contacted police who ran a check on the alleged deaconess. They found that religion had been used as a front for a scheme to ensnare girls into prostitution. The said deaconess was a known madam who sold girls she lured to a San Francisco white slave dealer for $300 apiece.

Young women had to beware. There were tales of girls pulled into automobiles by people asking for directions, never to be seen again. Theaters, too, were dangerous. Someone could sit down next to a young lady and, in the dark, apply ether to a handkerchief and put it over her mouth and nose. When she breathed she would pass out. The culprit would act as if she had fainted and claim he was helping her outside to get some fresh air.

In order to protect young women, and guard against immoral and unbecoming conduct on the beach during the evening, a powerful search light was installed upon the Sun Parlor in Long Beach to scan the sands at night for amorous couples. But what about the men who preyed upon unsuspecting women? Sometimes women got their revenge.

On the morning of September 21, 1918, the dead body of 43-year-old Frank S. Love, a Long Beach contractor, was found wrapped in canvas in an automobile near Compton, a bullet hole in his head. He had been returning home to Long Beach from his job painting the Girls' Collegiate School in Los Angeles. Those who saw him leave the school said he was alone. But could he have picked someone up along the way? A watch, money and jewelry were still on the body indicating that robbery was not the motive.

His wife, Carrie Love, said her husband told her he would be late coming home from Los Angeles because he wanted to visit a sick friend. However, when told of his death the following morning she did not seem concerned that he hadn't come home that night. She was happily packing provisions to take with them to Camp Baldy that afternoon; Frank was supposed to go with them, but he hadn't come home. Why wasn't she worried? Was she too embarrassed to mention his affairs and frequent late nights? Had she killed him?

She told reporters her husband had no enemies, as far as she knew. He was a pleasant, agreeable man, whom everyone seemed to like. But she was wrong. A fellow contractor had made threats against Love's life, accusing him of having an affair with his wife. Witnesses later told police they had seen a woman passenger in Love's car the evening of his murder arguing with Love; it had not been his wife. Police interviewed several women known to have been "special friends" of Love's, but all had satisfactory alibis. Police were certain there was a woman, maybe two, in the case responsible for Love's murder: a pair of women's gloves had been found in the automobile. They did not belong to Carrie Love. The police believed that after the shooting the car was driven to a meadow near Compton where an effort was made to clean the vehicle and the body deposited along the road. The deserted auto was found eight miles away; the exact place of the murder remained a mystery.

A murderer, or murderess, was never found.

More than Business Partners?

On January 14, 1914, the bodies of Mrs. Viola A. Kerr and Arthur E. Cunningham were lying at the J.J. Mottell undertaking parlor side by side, just as they had been the previous evening on a lonely spot on Willow Road near the outskirts of Long Beach. Indications were that Cunningham, after a desperate struggle, had shot the woman twice, and then turned the gun upon himself.

Thirty-nine-year-old Viola Kerr and thirty-six-year-old Arthur Cunningham were partners in a Long Beach real estate business which Mrs. Kerr had started six months earlier. Viola, the senior partner, had a reputation of being a hustling business woman, active in the community. She was also the mother of twin boys, seniors in high school. Her husband, Kelly Kerr, had no indication of any romance between his wife and Cunningham and said he would have trusted her anywhere with the man. Mrs. Cunningham, however, told a different story.

Two months before the suicide-murder Effie Cunningham told her husband he must choose between her and Viola. He laughed in her face. After this confrontation Mrs. Cunningham said her husband began to drink heavily and remained away from home much of the time. He also bought a gun, saying if Kelly Kerr found him with Viola he'd be able to defend himself.

The day of the tragedy the partners had been at their office and everything seemed fine. Colleagues said they saw nothing in the way the couple behaved to arouse even the remotest suspicion that there had been anything wrong going on between them. The day of the murder-suicide they had traveled together to San Pedro for business. When they returned to Long Beach Viola pulled the car over to the side of the road and evidence pointed to a quarrel. Beer bottles in the car indicated that Cunningham, if not Viola, had been drinking. As Viola sat at the wheel and Cunningham on the seat beside her, he reached over, drew her head to his breast and shot twice. She was still alive as he shot a third bullet through her heart. Then he turned the gun on himself; he fired at his head, but missed. The second bullet found its mark.

How long they sat upright in the car at the side of the road was anyone's guess. Many later admitted to passing the car and seeing a woman with her head on a man's shoulder. Someone finally notified the police. Police officers surmised that the only possible motive for the murder-suicide was that Cunningham, knowing his wife, parents and friends were aware of his infatuation for his charming partner, had brought his romance to a climax, and that he attempted to force Viola Kerr to run away with him. When she refused, he killed her and then himself.

Kelly Kerr still didn't believe his wife's relationship with Cunningham extended beyond business, nor did her friends who ardently defended her character. Kerr knew that Cunningham was a drinker and used liquor to drown his sorrow, but Kelly Kerr never knew what Cunningham's sorrow was. Cunningham's father said there no financial problems. Effie Cunningham, however, believed in an affair and told her husband she wanted to end their 13 year marriage. Perhaps it was the prospect of a divorce and lack of freedom to marry Viola that prompted his actions. But we'll never know. He took his reasons to the grave with him.

Murderous Sons

The mention of Long Beach always inspired a tongue-in-cheek attitude among the more sophisticated inlanders. Santa Monica made no secret of being a roaring resort, where one could enjoy the seashore with a glass of beer and revel in non-Victorian activities. Long Beach, with its strict ban on liquor and Sunday closing of most stores, was regarded as the seaside resort for the more conservative element. Since 1884, when the Long Beach Land Company donated four blocks of land to the Methodist Resort Association for camp meetings, Long Beach had been known as a town believing in and promoting religious ideals. From that time on it had tried to live up to that reputation. Though some made fun of temperate Long Beach, others were attracted to the town for that reason alone.

Many came to Long Beach seeking rest and solace at the Long Beach Sanitarium. The Dibert family from Topeka, Kansas, was one of those hoping for respite from their woes.

The $60,000 Long Beach Sanitarium (which later became St. Mary's Hospital) opened in June 1906. Patients flocked to its doors. All were impressed by its modernity and treatment. Mrs. Dibert had recently lost her husband and was worried about her 20-year-old son, Scott. The burden of handling her late husband's estate and her own ill health had fallen on the young man. Being involved in a traffic accident was the last straw for Scott Dibert; his behavior became so irrational he had to be institutionalized. Mrs. Dibert's older son, Ammon, asked that she come and live with him in Southern California where he could look after her and handle her finances. He suggested a quiet stay at the Long Beach Sanitarium where she could rest and recover from her physical as well as stress related illnesses. Mrs. Dibert, however, refused to leave her youngest son behind. She insisted Scott be released from the mental asylum and be allowed to accompany her to California. She was sure a stay at the sanitarium would help both of them. Besides, she was confident his older brother Ammon could look after him. She was wrong.

Though the evening of January 19, 1913, was brisk and wintry, Ammon Dibert thought the cool air and the soothing sound of waves breaking against the pier would help calm his brother's nerves. Scott had again been acting irrationally, perhaps from the stress brought on by their mother's deteriorating health. Scott was also insisting he attend to her finances, suspicious his older brother was skimming money from the estate. Ammon was not sure how to handle his brother's paranoia, but was trying to talk to him in a logical way. As they walked along the lower deck of the Pine Avenue Pier, Scott suddenly pulled a gun from his pocket.

Distraught, Scott proceeded to shoot his thirty-year-old brother through the head. He then fired a bullet into his own brain. The first 38-calibre revolver bullet struck Ammon in the neck and ranged upward through the head and came out under the right eye. The other bullet entered Scott's right temple and lodged in his head. Ammon was able to make it to a nearby store and report the shooting; he then fell to the floor. Scott was found leaning over the pier rail and soon died.

Ammon survived. But he had a terrible chore to perform. It was up to him to notify his invalid mother of Scott's death and help appease her guilt in insisting Scott be released from a mental institution. If she had left him there Scott would still be alive and, possibly, on the road to recovery.

Another family that moved to Long Beach in June 1914 was the Clarkson family, from Wellsville, Missouri. They came because their son Jack had a problem. He was an alcoholic. In an alcoholic daze and fit of jealousy he had threatened to kill his sweetheart, Alpha Hudson. It was time for the family to find help. What better place to seek a cure than the city known for its temperance stance, sanitarium and new medical ideas?

The family settled into a house at Eleventh and Orizaba, close to the Long Beach Sanitarium. It was a brisk half-hour stroll from their house to a pretty flowered walk which led the way up to the sanitarium at Tenth and Linden. The soft green tones inside the parlor calmed guests as they read, chatted or played the piano. On the third floor was a beautiful roof garden and sun parlor, giving a sweeping view of the city, ocean and bay.

The Long Beach Sanitarium was on the list of "must see" stops for tourists. Several times a day tour companies brought visitors to view the marvels the sanitarium offered. They gawked at the treatment rooms, where clients took invigorating baths and received massage therapies, and were amazed at the static room where electricity was used in treatments. Many families lived at the sanitarium for months at a time while one, or several, members regained their health. To accommodate the religious education of the young, there was a Sunday school and various devotional exercises practiced throughout the day. During evenings residents were treated to lectures such as "The Evil Effects of Stimulants and Narcotics." This is just what Alice Clarkson had been seeking for her son Jack.

The Long Beach Sanitarium used the "Battle Creek" idea, practiced by John H. Kellogg. At his Michigan sanitarium Kellogg advocated total abstinence from alcoholic beverages, tea, coffee, chocolate, tobacco, and condiments. He preached a meat free diet and believed milk, cheese, eggs, and refined sugars should be used sparingly, if at all. Man's natural foods, Kellogg claimed, were nuts, fruits, legumes and whole grains. He held that the best medicine was a reformed diet, sensible clothing, correct posture, and a program of regular exercise and rest, with liberal exposure to fresh air and sunshine. Alice had also read about Long Beach's own health guru, Dr. H.S. Tanner. If the sanitarium treatment didn't help her son, perhaps Dr. Tanner could. Tanner believed there was a deeper meaning to the Bible's account of Jesus' forty day fast in the desert. It was Tanner's belief Jesus was trying to show mankind the health benefits of fasting. After 33 years of research Tanner came up with his forty days' fasting cure. People flocked from all over the country to take his treatment.

The May 1909 article Alice had read discussed Dr. Tanner and the ten people fasting under his direction. Among them was E.P. Smith of Los Angeles, who had gained fame by writing 19,000 words on the back of a government post card. Guy H. Parkinson of 642 Pacific Avenue in Long Beach was also under Tanner's care. On May 18, 1909, Parkinson broke the world's fasting record set by Tanner, by abstaining from food for 43 days. What was remarkable was that Parkinson, a house mover, worked at his strenuous job almost every day of the fast without suffering loss of stamina or energy.

For a few months each year the San Francisco based Fer-Don European Medical Experts visited Long Beach to help people regain their health through bloodless surgery. Alice had also read about this group. She was happy the conscientious citizens and doctors of Long Beach had found out Fer-Don was a fake and his scheme a scam. This thoroughness in checking out health claims endeared Long Beach even more to Alice Clarkson, whose own health was fading. She was very pleased with her new home and confident that Jack would be cured of his alcohol addiction.

However, Jack was not happy. His mother rarely let him out of her sight, convinced he'd turn to the bottle once more. He wondered if she faked her own ill health just to tether him in even more. Most of all he worried why his sweetheart he left behind in Missouri didn't write back to him. He saw only one way out of his troubles. On April 16, 1915, he decided to commit suicide. But before he did he decided to murder his mother.

J.B. Clarkson had been dozing in the bedroom when he heard the sound of a gun. He leaped up and met his son, who still clasped a smoking revolver, in the hall. Jack was also clutching two sealed letters in his other hand. Jack's father immediately saw the body of his wife and tremulously asked his son if he was going to kill him as well. "No, father, I am not going to kill you. I have shot mother and I am going to kill myself. Here are two letters I want you to deliver." (*LA Times* 4/17/1915). Jack then went into the kitchen where he pointed the muzzle of the revolver to his forehead and pulled the trigger. The elder Clarkson, though stunned, somehow managed to rush from the house and call for help.

In one letter, addressed to his father, Jack wrote:

"I take mother with me and go myself because I know I am going and don't want her to be tortured. Now, please give us a nice burial. I have over $200 in the bank."

In the letter to Miss Alpha Hudson was the following:

"Alpha, I know you have been told that I pack a gun to kill you, but it is not so."

Jack killed his mother, his father believed, because he thought she could not live without him. J.B. Clarkson said there were few sons as devoted to his mother as Jack had been. He had nursed his bedridden mother over the last few months and it seemed she worried constantly when Jack was out of her sight.

Clarkson arranged for both bodies to be sent back to Missouri. Here, he hoped, Alpha would forgive his son for the troubles he had caused her. Then, perhaps, Jack could rest in peace.

Insane and Save from the Law?

On the evening of Saturday, October 24, 1908, retired Long Beach merchant Edward Bouman was en route home when he was held up and murdered. Before he died Bouman gave a meager description of his assailant, but the depiction led nowhere. Finally, a widow who ran a boarding house within a block of where the killing took place came forth with a possible suspect.

The woman told police she had rented a room to a young man named J. Lynn Otis, who didn't seem to have a job. He left his rooms at 9 o'clock each night and returned between 3 and 4 o'clock in the morning. He never left his room during the day. The night of Bouman's murder Otis didn't return until two days later; he was dirty, dusty and utterly worn out. He began packing his trunk and shaved off his beard. The next morning he told his landlady he was going away for two weeks, and paid his room rent two weeks in advance to hold it. He was very nervous, she reported. While his trunk was being loaded on a wagon he anxiously pulled a revolver from his pocket, extracted an empty shell and reloaded the weapon.

Otis' strange actions, coupled with the fact that several mysterious robberies had been committed in the neighborhood recently, led the police to examine the vacated room. Here they found various burglars' tools, consisting of window openers, files and jimmies. They also found a short, light overcoat, a black cap with a long visor and a face mask. Several rolls of bandages were also found and two vials wrapped in cotton. A chemist later identified the contents as nitro-glycerin. Several cartridges were also found in the room and one empty shell. Upon talking to the station master at the train depot authorities learned Otis had purchased a ticket to Denver.

After consulting with the district attorney the sheriff sent a telegram to Denver giving a description of Otis, his ticket number and the number of his trunk check, secured from the railroad. But Otis never arrived at Denver. His trunk went through to Colorado Springs. It was continuously watched, hoping Otis would show up to claim it. Several weeks later the station agent received instructions to forward the trunk to Dundee, New York. Long Beach police communicated with New York authorities only to find that Otis was incarcerated in the Willard State Insane Asylum, a raving maniac. The telegram stated that Otis was taken from a train at Ogden, Utah, suffering from dementia, and had been brought to New York by his brother, a physician of Dundee, and committed.

New York authorities said they tried to talk to Otis about Bouman's murder, but every time either Long Beach or Bouman's name was mentioned Otis began to rave or else became morose and sullen. The verdict was he was hopelessly insane, too crazy to be put on trial for murder. Had money and his doctor brother's verdict saved Otis from prison, or was he truly insane?

Can insanity keep you safe from the law? The insanity defense is one of the most controversial of all criminal defense strategies which, put simply, asserts that people who are insane cannot have the intent required to perform a criminal act because they either did not know the act was wrong or could not control their actions even when they understood the act was wrong. Defendants found to be insane are committed to mental hospitals rather than prisons, where they can be confined for longer than their actual prison terms would have been. But some mental institutions are more like country clubs and are definitely preferable to jail, as the case of Harry K. Thaw exemplifies.

On January 9, 1917, one of America's most infamous men, Harry K. Thaw, slayer of renowned architect Stanford White, was named in a New York grand jury indictment as the kidnapper and torturer of a 19-year-old Long Beach youth, Frederick Gump, Jr.

Thaw was a railroad millionaire from Pittsburgh, Pennsylvania, married to vivacious entertainer Evelyn Nesbit. Stanford White and Evelyn Nesbit had met and carried on an affair despite the watchful eye of her jealous husband. But Thaw eventually did find out about the romantic trysts of the pair. On June 25, 1906, Thaw met Stanford White in Madison Square Garden, shooting and killing him before a stunned crowd. The murder, and subsequent trial, was front page news throughout the world. Thaw's defense was temporary insanity as a result of White's seduction of his wife.

In April 1907 the jury in the Stanford White murder trial declared it could not reach a verdict, and a second trial began in January 1908. The following month Thaw was found not guilty on the grounds of insanity and sentenced to the Asylum for the Criminal Insane at Matteawan, New York. Thaw was released from Matteawan in June 1915 after being declared sane (a verdict helped by money from his mother to New York authorities). Soon after Mother Thaw, as everyone called her, brought her son along on a trip to Long Beach to visit her brother Josiah Copley. Here he met Frederick Gump Jr. in an ice cream parlor.

A short time after Thaw's Long Beach visit his divorce from Nesbit was finalized. Mother Thaw had seen to everything. She promised Evelyn that if Evelyn testified White had raped her and that Thaw had only tried to avenge her honor, Evelyn would receive a quiet divorce and a million dollar settlement. Evelyn received the divorce, but not the money.

Now, in 1917, Harry Thaw was in the news again in a bizarre story of kidnapping and torture. The nation was once more captivated by the tale of the crazy, murderous millionaire who thought he could escape justice. They eagerly read how Thaw had lured Frederick Gump, Jr. to New York with promises of a scholarship to Carnegie Institute. Gump had arrived on Christmas Eve and Thaw had assured him of a very memorable Christmas. It was unforgettable, but not what young Frederick had expected. Perhaps the eggnog Frederick was served was drugged for somehow Thaw managed to tie the young man up. He then proceeded to beat Frederick severely.

Armed with two whips, one of which was knotted, Thaw lashed Frederick for more than an hour, while the boy fought vainly to escape. Finally Frederick fell to the floor, weak and exhausted. He pleaded for mercy. Thaw made the boy kneel on the floor and kiss Thaw's toes, hands, cheeks and lips, forcing him to repeat after him "I am your slave for four years. You are my master; I will obey your orders."

At breakfast the next morning Thaw, with the whips always at hand, forced the boy to kneel by his side while he fed him with his hands. After each mouthful Frederick was made to say "Thank you, master." Following breakfast another young man came into the room. Thaw gave the boy $10 and told the boy to take Frederick out for a walk. Frederick managed to escape with the $10 and caught a street car for the railroad station, where he boarded a train to return home. He was sure that with Thaw's money to bribe authorities, his story would never be believed. His parents, however, convinced him to go to the authorities and report his almost unbelievable tale. (*LA Times* 1/12/1917)

Frederick's grandfather, John, who owned a postcard business in Long Beach, told reporters his grandson had met Thaw when the millionaire was in Long Beach in October 1915. Thaw had originally come to California with his mother to attend the Panama-Pacific Exposition at San Francisco then traveled south to Long Beach to visit Mother Thaw's brother. Frederick Gump, Jr. met Harry Thaw while working as a fountain clerk at the Arbor on the Pike. Gump, the newspapers reported, had facial features which greatly resembled those of Evelyn Nesbit, Thaw's soon-to-be ex-wife. Thaw, it was said, dropped in often to see Frederick, and expressed a friendship for the boy.

Newspaper accounts of Thaw's trial, his wife's testimony and his mother's money, combined with his certifiable insanity, made Harry K. Thaw into an American hero, a celebrity sure to impress a young man like Frederick Gump, Jr. Later the two carried on a correspondence. Following his graduation from Poly High School in 1916, Frederick accepted Thaw's offer to visit him in New York and discuss the scholarship Thaw promised him. That was when Thaw's aberrant behavior began.

To prevent Thaw's extradition from Pittsburgh to New York on Frederick's kidnapping/assault charges, Mother Thaw arranged to have a Pennsylvania commission on lunacy again judge Harry Thaw insane. He was committed to the Pennsylvania State Hospital in Philadelphia. Here he stayed for seven years, until 1924.

Tiring of life in the asylum, where he had a great deal of freedom, Thaw decided he would like to leave Pennsylvania for a change of scenery. Mother Thaw thought it would be good politics to settle the $650,000 in damages claimed by the Gump family before another sanity trial was held on her son's release. In 1924, with the help of good lawyers, Mary Thaw was able to get the Gumps to settle for $25,000. The sanity trial was duly held; Harry K. Thaw was again declared sane. His property was restored and all his legal rights.

Frederick came back to Long Beach where he met Minnie Krick. The two married in October 1923. Money received in the settlement with Thaw was invested by the family in local real estate.

Thaw's legal troubles were not over. In 1929 he was sued for beating a woman, Marcia Estardus, a nightclub hostess. After three trials she was awarded $16,000 in damages. With the death of his mother, Mary, in June 1929, Thaw had only himself, and $40 million, to get him out of trouble. Somehow, he managed to behave himself until he suffered a fatal heart attack in Miami, Florida on February 22, 1947. He was 76.

Thaw was survived by his son, Russell William Thaw, born in 1910 during Thaw's confinement. Thaw always claimed Russell, who looked just like Nesbit, was not his child. Nesbit said otherwise. She finally gave up trying to seek justice. "A working girl could not fight the Thaw millions," she told the press *(LA Times 5/20/1924)*. During Evelyn Nesbit's remaining years she overcame suicide attempts, morphine addition and alcoholism. She died in a nursing home in Santa Monica on January 17, 1967, at the age of 82.

Coincidental Murders?

Two strikingly similar murders involving domestic disputes and suicide occurred in Long Beach in March 1919.

On March 20, 1919, Oliver Nelson, proprietor of a restaurant on the Pike, fatally shot his wife Cora, and then took his own life. Nelson had arranged to meet his estranged wife at the Pacific Electric station in East Long Beach and discuss their marital situation. Two times she had stood him up. Perhaps she had a premonition that something was not right. She finally relented and agreed to meet him on neutral territory, with plenty of people around them.

As the Red Car came into the Zaferia station Oliver Nelson spotted his wife waiting for him on the platform. She had arrived earlier on a car from Huntington Beach. Angrily he approached her, demanding a good reason why she had stood him up two times earlier. As the yelling worsened, a shrieking Cora Nelson picked up her umbrella and struck Oliver repeatedly over the head with it until it broke from the blows. Nelson then drew a 32-calibre revolver from his pocket and fired three shots at her as she ran away. She might have saved her life if she hadn't fallen while crossing the street car tracks. Her estranged husband caught up with her and, as she lay on the ground, shot her through her right temple. He then pointed the weapon at his temple and fired. His death was instantaneous.

Friends of Oliver Nelson believed the murder was planned. When saying goodbye to some acquaintances, Nelson intimated they wouldn't be seeing him again. This theory of premeditation was strengthened by the fact that Nelson carried two loaded revolvers to the scene of the shooting. Friends said the couple had been separated for at least six months. Nelson, some twenty years older than his 45-year-old wife, was jealous. The couple had been married eight years.

On March 30, 1919, Gilbert W. Hatfield, a 45-year-old Long Beach shipyard worker, shot and killed his 31-year-old wife, Lena, and then committed suicide on the corner of Fifth and Locust. Lena, who worked at a local ice cream parlor, had recently sued for divorce. Hatfield, wanting reconciliation, confronted his wife as she was returning to her parent's home where she had been living since the couple separated.

C.G. Davis was in his backyard on Locust Avenue when the Hatfields walked by. They were quarreling, he told police, and Hatfield seemed angry because his wife refused to listen to his arguments about coming back to live with him. As Lena started to run away, Hatfield opened fire. The first bullet struck the woman in the arm, knocking her down. Hatfield then fired two more bullets into her back at close range. He then shot himself in the head.

Long Beach police officer Claude Robberson just couldn't help but notice the similarities in the two cases. The Hatfields like the Nelsons had been separated several months prior to the tragedy. Both men attempted reconciliation with their wives, but in both instances failed. Both murders were preceded by quarrels. Both women were shot as they attempted to flee from their husbands. In both instances as the women fell their husbands rushed up and at close range fired the fatal bullets. Both men shot the same number of times, and in each case the same caliber of revolver was used. The husbands of the two women shot themselves in the same place, the temple, and both died instantly while their wives lingered a short time upon arriving at the same hospital. Other strange coincidences connected with the cases included the fact that both women were younger than their husbands, both women were former residents of Huntington Beach, both had been married before, and both had a son and daughter by their previous marriage.

Claude Robberson, the police officer who noted the similarities in both murders, went on to become assistant Long Beach police chief and later Chief of Police for the City of Ontario. Was it coincidence that his death echoed that of Gilbert Hatfield and Oliver Nelson? On August 27, 1949, the 58-year-old retired policeman shot and killed himself in his home at 1747 Cherry Avenue in Long Beach. Ironically, he shot himself in the temple like Nelson and Hatfield, dying instantly. Though he too had a younger wife, it seemed a money problem, not marriage difficulties, was the cause behind his death.

Killer Cats

Unbelievably, it seemed the new 1914 Long Beach charter made it mandatory to regulate the speed of cats within the city limits and require them to have fenders. The copy of the charter as passed by State officials contained many clerical errors. One of them made Long Beach responsible for the speed of cats. Section 21 of article 2 of the charter provided that the speed of railway trains, cats and engines be regulated. Too many fatal accidents had occurred because of excessive speed. Of course the intent of the charter was that "cars" and not "cats" be regulated as to speed, but the copy of the charter passed by the legislature legally placed the animals on the regulation list.

The media had a field day with Long Beach's misprint. Taking part in the fun, Mayor Louis Whealton told the press he thought City Clerk Harry B. Riley should be appointed to enforce the cat-speeding limit since he was the one who hadn't corrected the typing mistake. The Long Beach mayor went on to offer a prize of $10 to the person writing the most humorous news clip on the regulation of the speed of cats. The following appeared in the March 8, 1915, *Los Angeles Times*:

> *"A handsome Angora cat belonging to Mrs. Albert Laughrin was taken into custody yesterday on a charge of exceeding the cat speed limit. The case of*

'Betsy' will be made a test one, according to police officers. If she is convicted it is darkly hinted that all of her nine lives will go out simultaneously.

On Ocean Avenue and First Street the hotels are so close together that the roofs make one continuous speedway for innumerable cats. The Long Beach "cat cops," have endeavored to take these marauding and musical felines alive in vain, and they are determined to act in accordance with the new cat-speed law, and shoot the cats on the wing, where they can later testify to excessive speed.

In regard to the fenders, which the charter specifies should be placed on cats, city officials are divided. Some think that life nets placed in front of the tabbies would be just the thing to protect life and limb. Others are of the opinion that it would lessen the much desired mortality among rats and mice. Would it be easy for a mouse to escape the maw of the house cat, once he is scooped up in the fender?"

Not all found this frivolity over cats funny. Cats could be a nuisance.

W.L. Jennings of 232 Maine St. was a good neighbor. He frequently helped his widowed neighbor, Elizabeth Shaeffer, when she needed work done around her house. He was a little taken aback, however, when she asked him to kill her cat.

Mr. Jennings and his family were walking out the door to go to the movies on September 17, 1916, when their elderly neighbor came in with her request. It seemed the cat had been giving her all sorts of problems—getting into the breakfast dishes, leaping onto the table to steal food and scratching furniture. It was also full of fleas which infested her small apartment. She had tried to shoo the cat away, make it find another home, but the cat kept coming back, sometimes even bringing her "gifts" such as a dead bird or rat. It had adopted her, even though she didn't want a cat; she barely had enough money to buy food for herself let alone a cat. She was extremely distraught. The only recourse, it seemed, was to kill the cat.

Jennings sent his wife and three children on to the theater. He thought it best that his children not be around when he performed the deadly deed. He suggested that Mrs. Shaeffer accompany the family to the movies and told them he would join them shortly. But he never got to the theater. When he failed to appear his wife assumed the "chore" had taken longer than he had thought. She had a big surprise awaiting her when she returned home. She found her husband dead.

Jennings' face was buried in a chloroform-soaked quilt, which covered a bucket in which he had placed the cat. The feline was nowhere to be found. It seemed that Jennings, bending over the quilt which covered the pail from which the cat escaped, absorbed so much of the chloroform that he fell forward, burying his face in the quilt. Breathing the fumes, he died. Was the cat a killer of not only feathered creatures and rodents, but of Mr. Jennings?

Not all thought cats a nuisance. There was one man who would kill to protect his beloved feline.

Being a fisherman could be lonely, as William Oliver would later testify. Out by himself all day with only his cat to come home to, Oliver found the companionship of his cat more desirable than that of his closest neighbor, "Mexican Joe." Though Oliver lovingly shared his catch with his feline friend, his cat often preferred food with more fiber and tang. The cat would satisfy his longing for a different cuisine by going to Joe's house and helping himself to Joe's spicier food. Joe was not happy with these feline visits and raids on his larder and had tossed the cat into the water a time or two. Still, the cat came back.

On the evening of November 6, 1918, the cat was dining at Joe's when Joe walked in. He picked the animal up and gave it a throw. William Oliver, out searching for his feline friend, observed the confrontation. Angered at what he considered the brutal treatment of his favorite pet, he fired a gun at his 60-year-old Anaheim Landing neighbor. The bullet went through Joe's left arm and into his body. Somehow Joe managed to make it to another neighbor's house and tell what had happened before he died.

After the murder Oliver fled to Elsinore where he got a job cutting wood. Later, thinking the law had given up searching for him, he ventured into nearby Santa Ana. The 5-foot 7-inch tall, 168 pound man was identified by his gray eyes, brown and gray hair, deep scar on his right cheek and heavily tattooed arms. Thrown in jail, he later battered a hole in the wall of his cell with the side of his bed. He was taken to the Orange County Hospital for psychiatric observation.

On January 29, 1919, the 46-year-old fisherman escaped from the hospital clad only in black and white striped pajamas and a pair of socks. His trail led eastward toward Orange and officers believed he was heading towards Elsinore, where he had some additional clothing. Several days later Oliver was apprehended. He told police he had escaped because Mexicans were planning to break into the hospital and kill him. At his trial in April 1919 William Oliver was judged insane and committed to the Norwalk asylum for the criminally insane.

No word on what happened to the cat.

Index

Buchanon, S.J. 61-62
Bunch, George 28-29
Burrell, B.A. 91
Bush, Clement C. 98

C

California Supreme Court SEE Courts,
    California Supreme
Carroll Park 114
Carson, George 15
Castello, Nicholas 57-59
Castle, Clara 83-84
Castle, Olin 82-84
Castro, Bernardino 42-43
Catalina Island 52, 78
Cats 153-156
Cemeteries
  Evergreen 56, 67
  Municipal 5, 60, 70, 78, 80-81, 120
  Sunnyside 95
Chafor, George E. 97
Chapman, Ervin 16
Charles, Henry 28
Chautauqua 16, 18-19, 53, 54
Chavez, Jacinto 49
City Council 97, 105 SEE ALSO City
    Trustees
City Hall 101, 104, 106
City Marshal 2, 22, 37, 59, 101 SEE
    ALSO Police
City Trustees 5, 6, 8, 17-22 SEE ALSO
    City Council
Civil War 70, 116, 126
Clark, James 38, 39, 89
Clark, William 38, 39, 89
Clarkson, Alice 140, 141-143
Clarkson, Jack 140, 142-143
Cochran, Emmett 60-61
Collins, Roscoe 91
Colorado 13, 39, 145
Compton 39, 47, 134, 135
Cook, Jennie 49-51
Coolidge, Warren T. 59
Copley, Josiah 146

Cort, Daisy 108-110
Coseboom, Clarence 18, 19
Coughran, Clinton 43-44
Courts
  California Supreme 19, 20, 97, 98
  Municipal 19, 20
  Superior 96, 97
Cunningham, Arthur E. 136-137
Cunningham, Effie 136, 137
Cycling 68-71

D

Dane, Hiram 126
Davis, "Whistling" 2-4
Davis, C.G. 151
Denio, E.C. 19
Deshazer, Alvin 91
DeVoe, Steve 116
De Ball Ranch 41
De talent, Lillian 82
Diaz, Juan 31
Dibert, Ammon 139
Dibert, Scott 138-140
Disincorporation 6, 19-21
Dominguez, Benito 42
Dominguez Rancho SEE Ranchos,
    Dominguez
Donatelli, Nicola 84-86
Downey 104
Doyle, Frank 14
Drake, Charles 56-57, 89-90
Drownings 54-59, 126
Dunn, J.C. 19

E

Earthquakes 92, 114
East Long Beach SEE Zaferia
Elections 19, 20, 21
Elikan, Camille 9-13
Embezzlement 72, 110
Empire Day 92-98
Encinal, Esiquito 48, 49
Encinal, Gregorio 48
Esalenta, Joseph 33-34

L

Labourdette, Pete 30, 33, 37, 38, 39-40
LaFetra, Milton 49
Laws SEE Ordinances
Leavenworth SEE Prisons, Leavenworth
Ledesma, Jose 41
Lemas, Jose 40-41
Lew-is the Light 72, 76-77
Lilley, Constance 118-120
Linson, Irvin 14
Lipscomb, George 61
Long, J. Howard 56
Long Beach Hotel. SEE Hotels, Long Beach
Long Beach Land and Water Company 4
Long Beach Police SEE Police
Long Beach Sanitarium.103, 138, 139, 140-141 SEE ALSO Hospitals
Long Beach Trustees SEE City Trustees
Lopez, Alegos 40-41
Lopez, Manuel 37
Lopez, Rosallo 33
Los Alamitos, City of 30, 32, 37-40, 43-44
Los Alamitos Rancho SEE Ranchos, Los Alamitos
Los Angeles, City of 2, 9, 10, 16, 19, 29, 37, 39, 45, 46, 47, 49, 50, 54, 56, 66, 67, 72, 73, 74, 75, 77, 95, 99, 103, 104, 111, 112, 114, 116, 117, 122, 134, 135, 141
Los Angeles County 3, 19, 20, 21, 22, 25, 26, 77, 101, 104, 105
Los Cerritos Rancho SEE Ranchos, Los Cerritos
Love, Carrie 135
Love, Frank S. 134-135
Lowe, Belle 10, 12, 13
Lowe, Ethel 9-13
Lowe, William 10, 11, 13
Loynes, Richard 87

M

Machado, Jose 27-28
Magnolia Avenue Pier SEE Piers, Magnolia Avenue
Majestic Skating Rink 82, 86
McCarthy, Dennis 6, 16, 17-18, 20-22
McKee, Dorothy 68-71, 87
McPherson, Anna 100
McPherson, Joseph 6-7, 16
Mendoza, Lucas 31
Meteer, John H. 99
Methever, Edward 68-71
Methever, Ulysses 71
Methodists 54, 73, 74, 82, 98-100, 131, 138
Mexicans 8-9, 25, 30-33, 35, 37, 40-43, 45, 47-49, 91, 116, 125, 128, 155-156
Mexico 8, 30, 31, 33, 60, 61, 66
Meyers, Alonzo 13-15
Meyers, Mabel 13-15
Miller, H.J. 78, 79
Mining 24, 28, 33, 39, 60, 72, 114
Missouri 5, 71, 73, 75, 140, 142, 143
Mitchell, Gerard 66-67
Montana 39, 61, 62, 72, 73, 75
Morales, Sylvestro 26-30
Moreno, Ricardo 8-9, 17
Morillo, Francisco 32-33
Morris, G.T. 59-60
Morrison, Jessie 83-84
Morro, Luciano 31
Moyer, Clarence 102, 103, 116, 117
Mundy, Hendrick 99, 100
Municipal Auditorium 93-98
Municipal Cemetery SEE Cemeteries, Municipal
Musicians 82, 84, 85, 86, 108. SEE ALSO Bands
Myers, Al 112-114

N

Native Americans 30, 47
Neece, Milton F. 80

160

Y

Z

CPSIA information can be obtained at www.ICGtesting.com
Printed in the USA
BVOW011704231111

276717BV00001B/9/P